Unbearable Cost

Unbearable Cost

Bush, Greenspan and the Economics of Empire

James K. Galbraith

First published 2006 by
PALGRAVE MACMILLAN
Houndmills, Basingstoke, Hampshire RG21 6XS and
175 Fifth Avenue, New York, N.Y. 10010
Companies and representatives throughout the world

PALGRAVE MACMILLAN is the global academic imprint of the Palgrave
Macmillan division of St. Martin's Press, LLC and of Palgrave Macmillan Ltd.
Macmillan® is a registered trademark in the United States, United Kingdom
and other countries. Palgrave is a registered trademark in the European
Union and other countries.

ISBN 13: 978–0–230–01889–1   hardback
ISBN 10: 0–230–01889–0   hardback
ISBN 13: 978–0–230–01901–0   paperback
ISBN 10: 0–230–01901–3   paperback

This book is printed on paper suitable for recycling and made from fully
managed and sustained forest sources.

A catalogue record for this book is available from the British Library.

Library of Congress Cataloging-in-Publication Data

Galbraith, James K.
    Unbearable cost : Bush, Greenspan and the economics of empire /
by James K. Galbraith.
        p. cm.
    Includes bibliographical references and index.
    ISBN 0–230–01889–0 (cloth) – ISBN 0–230–01901–3 (pbk.)
        1. United States – Economic policy – 2001–2. United States – Politics
    and government – 2001– 3. Bush, George W. (George Walker), 1946–
    4. Greenspan, Alan, 1926– I. Title.

    HC106.83.G34 2007
    338.973–dc22   2006045599

10   9   8   7   6   5   4   3   2   1
15 14 13 12 11 10 09 08 07 06

Printed and bound in Great Britain by
Antony Rowe Ltd, Chippenham and Eastbourne

For Molly Ivins
Funnier Than Me

Contents

About War

About Greenspan

About the Economy

x *Contents*

Acknowledgments

I've been lucky to work for many years with editors of great talent, equally good at shaping thought and polishing prose. Among these I thank especially Bob Kuttner of *The American Prospect*, Sid Blumenthal during the year I contributed to *Salon*, Michael King, Lou Dubose, Nate Blakeslee, Jake Bernstein and Barbara Belejack in succession at the *Texas Observer*, Katrina Van den Heuvel and Karen Rothmyer at *The Nation*, Clara Jeffery at *Mother Jones*, Leland Montgomery during the bubble months with TheStreet.Com, Howard Goldberg at *The New York Times*, Jefferson Morley at *The Washington Post*, Spencer Rumsey at *Newsday*, Marjorie Pritchard at the *Boston Globe*, Ann Brenoff and Sue Horton at the *Los Angeles Times*, and Matthew Rothschild at *The Progressive*. None bear responsibility for any errors remaining here.

At the LBJ School of Public Affairs, my forays into short-form journalism were inspired by Barbara Jordan, warmly encouraged by Elspeth Rostow, and supported in the years covered here by my dean, Ed Dorn.

Great thanks to my agent, Wendy Strothman, and to Amanda Hamilton of Palgrave Macmillan who saw the interest in bringing these columns together into a book.

At home, I've had support, love and infinite patience from Ying Tang, the ever-enchanting diversions of life with Emma and Eve, and the affectionate solidarity of Maggie and Doug. Thanks and love in return to all.

In all literary matters, I owe more than I can say to the influence of my father, John Kenneth Galbraith, who died just as this book went to press. A master of the precise English phrase, he read many of these pieces on first publication and sent encouraging notes when he approved. His example and memory are my enduring inspiration.

Permissions

The figure accompanying 'Boom Times for War Inc.' is reprinted by kind permission of Claude Serfati and Luc Mampaey, 'Galbraith and institutionalist analysis: an assessment based on the US military-industrial system transformations in the 1990s', in *Innovation, Evolution and Economic Change: New Ideas in the Tradition of Galbraith*, eds Blandine Laperche, James K. Galbraith and Dimitri Uzunidis (2006).

I thank William K. Black, Michael D. Intriligator and George Purcell for kind permission to reprint coauthored material.

All other articles are either © James K. Galbraith, or reprinted here with the permission of the original publisher.

Introduction

These columns span a minor writing career: from the stolen election of 2000, through September 11, 2001 and onward to the war in Iraq. They end with the consolidation of Republican power in the flawed – not to say rigged – election of 2004. Thus they chronicle the decline of American democracy in the first term of George W. Bush.

Let's not romanticize American government before Bush. Elites largely controlled, then as now. But at the end of the day, though with many fits and starts, American governments of both parties did tend to feel the pressure of the people's will. The American public have an enduring wish for peace, for prosperity, and for continuity in the basic functions of the state, including social security, health, education and welfare. These governments have often neglected. But they have also known that if neglect goes too far, the voters will react in the end. And they have adjusted to that reality. Those of us with long memories can see, in retrospect, these qualities even in the governments of Nixon and Reagan, however much we loathed them when they were in power.

But government of this type is gone now. In its place, we have something different, something more single-minded in its purposes and unrestrained in its actions. Immediately after the George W. Bush installation I gave it a name: 'Corporate Democracy'. This is government not on the model of politics, but on the model of the corporation.

The form of government long established in the business realm was analyzed almost forty years ago by my father in *The New Industrial State*. It consists of a self-dealing Board of Directors and of a permanent management and technical apparatus – the technostructure. The essential task of the latter is to control all aspects of the business climate, from production to marketing, while suppressing, so far as possible, the conflicting interests of unionists, regulators, and the business competition. This form of government, in a word, is about *control*.

The Board and technostructure are attended by a public relations bureau with no particular allegiance to the truth. The PR bureau speaks to the financial press, which treats its emissions with the deference due to men of substance and power. Thus constraints of veracity and consistency are neither imposed nor respected. There are elections, from time to time. But these the management so arranges that the Board does not lose. I was in Columbus, Ohio in the first days of November, 2004; I observed first-hand how this now works in America.

Even when run on the business model, governments have powers going well beyond those of the corporation. Two of the most important are the power to make war and the power to print money. These form the topics of many of the pieces that follow here.

War is a major temptation of elites. William Niskanen, of the Cato Institute, makes the interesting suggestion that America tends to get into wars only when the White House and Congress are controlled by a single party. However that may be, Bush has gotten us into two of them so far: the 'Global War on Terror' and Iraq.

In the strict sense, the war on terror is a phony war. It is more of a phrase, a device for politics, rather than a major drain on national resources or on the military. We were hit on September 11, and we fought a lightning campaign, largely successful, to kick Al Qaeda and the Taliban out of power in Afghanistan. Since then, there have been no more attacks – yet – on American soil, and Al Qaeda's terrorism has been of a conventional sort, mostly in or near the Muslim homelands. It is now clear that 9/11 did not presage a crippling war on American soil – any more than Pearl Harbor presaged an actual Japanese invasion of the United States. We fight the war on terror, in other words, with small forces in remote places, and otherwise largely in our own minds.

The war in Iraq, on the other hand, is all too real. It is a war with over 2200 Americans dead so far, alongside uncounted tens of thousands of Iraqis, and no end in sight. And it illustrates the true character of modern imperial wars. They are easy to get into, hard to get out of, and far more expensive than their advocates imagine. This much was visible to an economist from the beginning. It was, in particular, visible to me, as a student for many years of the costs of war. And I so warned at the time.

It is an unfailing feature of American debates over wars that the costs are never seriously considered beforehand. They only become decisive after they have been incurred. Before the war, the arguments of accountants lose out to the romantics: to the world changers and the spreaders of freedom. Only afterward does the public become concerned with the problem of costs. By then, of course, it is too late to undo the damage. Economists, who are not normally the most useful people, should enjoy more influence in this area. It is one of the few where we enjoy insights of real importance. My columns on the problem of war and its costs state facts and associations that were known at the time. But they did not enter into decision and debate when it mattered.

Alan Greenspan has been a topic of mine for many years; my columns on him included here predate the Bush reign for that reason. They illustrate what I've called the Mexican Presidency theory of the Federal Reserve: an organization whose chairmen are considered prophets while in office and non-entities afterward. Greenspan understands this, which explains in part why he stayed around so long.

And over almost twenty years on the job, Greenspan had his good moments. Most exceptionally, he did nothing for four years in the late 1990s, permitting the economy to reach a state of non-inflationary full employment. This, the overwhelming majority of the economics profession had derided, for years beforehand, as a technical impossibility. Greenspan's inaction therefore took considerable courage, patience and forbearance.

For these qualities, I give him credit. But other tendencies – his willingness to shill and toady for an administration of radical right-wing view and social irresponsibility, were also present all along. And they have come to coincide with the long economic decay that got underway in 2000. Therefore Greenspan's reputation declined even as he remained in office.

The money power compels interest for a deeper reason. The financial markets, or more precisely the great speculators who inhabit them, are the great predators of capitalism. And just as they devour the weak, ill-defended, or unlucky corporation, they have the potential to destabilize, undermine, or even occasionally destroy the government of the ill-defended state. Financial weakness is, therefore, possibly the Achilles heel of the new corporate state. Especially, those who seize power with imperial ambitions rarely understand the financial limits on military power. And there is no evidence that such understanding penetrated the upper reaches of the Bush administration in the run-up to the Iraq war.

Characteristically throughout history, the mismanagement of money is what turns imperial pretensions to dust. First comes the erosion of institutions that preserve the economic strength, purchasing power and security of the great mass of the public. This opens the door to speculative instability and to a frightened unwillingness in private business to spend, to invest, to live the life of economic expansion, opportunity and growth. Then comes the erosion of international finance. Sooner or later, the world at large withdraws the high privilege of borrowing in one's own currency. In this way, empires tend to crumble; the costs of empire have always proved unbearable in the end.

So it will prove, one suspects, for the present leaders of the United States. For the sixty years following World War II, we have stood in the world as the leader of freedom and prosperity – a unique combination of moral authority and economic might. With the end of the Cold War, it was necessary – we can see it now – that we reinvent our moral authority in order to preserve our economic might. We failed to do that. And while 'projects for the new American century' can be invented by those who understand nothing of economics or morals, they cannot succeed. Richard Nixon's chief economic adviser, Herbert Stein, was fond of saying that 'when a trend cannot continue, it will stop'. As a corollary, one might offer: when something is impossible, it won't happen.

About President George W. Bush as a person, I have little to say. In speeches before audiences at home, I have often described myself as a great follower of his. I followed him to Andover. I followed him to both Harvard and Yale. I followed him to Texas. And then I stopped. Mercifully, Texas is a large place. But my concern here is not with personality or past behavior, and readers looking for an attack on Bush's character will be disappointed. These essays are about the principles, the structures, and the conduct of government. They are about politics and policy – about peace, about jobs, and about elections that count and are counted. They are about the battles ahead, if we are someday to establish the real form of democracy in America, in place of the corporate version.

Austin, Texas, 21 March 2006

About Bush

Corporate Democracy; Civic Disrespect

With the events of late in the year 2000, the United States left behind constitutional republicanism, and turned to a different form of government. It is not, however, a new form. It is rather, a transplant, highly familiar from a different arena of advanced capitalism.

This is corporate democracy. It is a system whereby a Board of Directors – read Supreme Court – selects the Chief Executive Officer. The CEO in turn appoints new members of the Board. The shareholders are invited to cast their votes in periodic referenda. But the franchise is only symbolic, for management holds a majority of proxies. On no important issue do the CEO and the Board ever permit themselves to lose.

The Supreme Court clarified this in a way that the Florida courts could not have. The media have accepted it, for it is the form of government to which they are already professionally accustomed. And the shameless attitude of the Bush high command merely illustrates, in unusually visible fashion, the prevalence of this ethical system.

Gore's concession speech was justly praised for grace and humor. It paid due deference to the triumph of corporate political ethics, but did not embrace them. It thus preserved Gore for another political day. But Gore also sent an unmistakable message to American democrats: do not forget.

It was an important warning, for almost immediately forgetting became the order of the day. Overnight, it became almost un-American *not* to accept the *diktat* of the Court. Press references from that moment forward were to President-*elect* Bush, an unofficial title and something that the Governor from Texas (President-select? President-designate?) manifestly is not.

7

The key to dealing with the Bush people, however, is precisely not to accept them. Like most Americans, I have nothing personal against Bush, Cheney, nor against Colin Powell and the other members of the new administration. But I will not reconcile myself to them. They lost the election. Then they arranged to obstruct the count of the vote. They don't deserve to be there, and that changes everything. They have earned our civic disrespect, and that is what we, the people, should accord them.

Civic disrespect means that the illegitimacy of this administration must not be allowed to fade from view. The conventions of politics remain: Bush will be President; Congress must work with him. But those of us outside that process are not bound by those conventions, and to the extent that we have a voice we should use it.

Politically, civic disrespect means drawing lines around the freedom of maneuver of the incoming Administration. In some areas, including foreign policy, there may be few major changes; in others, such as annual budgets and appropriations, compromises will have to be reached. But Bush should be opposed on actions whose reach will extend beyond his actual term.

First, the new President should be allowed lifetime appointments only by consensus. The fifty Senate Democrats should freely block judicial nominations, whenever they carry even the slightest ideological taint. As for the Supreme Court especially, vacancies need not be filled.

Second, the Democrats should advise Bush not to introduce any legislation to cut or privatize any part of Social Security or Medicare.

Third, Democrats should furiously oppose elimination of the estate tax – a social incentive for recycling wealth that has had a uniquely powerful effect on the form of American society.

Fourth, we must oppose the global dangers of National Missile Defense – a strategic nightmare that threatens for all time the security of us all.

Fifth, Congress should enact a New Voting Rights Act, targeted precisely at the Florida abuses. This should stipulate mandatory adoption of best-practice technology; a 24-hour voting day; a ban on private contractors to aid in purging voter rolls; and mandatory immediate hand count of all under-votes in federal elections.

Further, Democrats must recognize and adapt to the new politics that emerged from this election. Outside of Florida, and facing a Southern Republican, the Democrats can't win the South. But they have excellent prospects of consolidating a narrow majority of the electoral college – so long as, in the next election, there is no Nader defection.

What can prevent such a thing? Only a move *away* from the main Clinton compromises that so infuriated the progressive left. Nader's voters were motivated passionately by issues like the drug war, the death penalty, consumer protection and national missile defense – issues where New Democrats took Republican positions, but failed to win Republican votes, while losing critical votes on the left.

Al Gore's campaign proved that there is a majority in the United States for a government that is truly a progressive coalition – and not merely an assemblage of sympathetic lawyers, professors and investment bankers. Rather, Americans will elect a government that includes and effectively represents labor, women, minorities – and greens. This is the government we must seek to elect – if we get another chance.

And for that, the first task is to assure that the information ministries of our new corporate republic do not successfully cast a fog of forgetting over the crime that we have all just witnessed, with our own eyes.

(*The Texas Observer*, 19 January 2001)

Lies, Dumb Lies, and Sample Statistics

The press has welcomed George W. Bush and well they might. Bush has freed them, at last, from the immense frustration of dealing with that compulsive liar, Bill Clinton.

The problem with Clinton's lies was not, of course, that they *were* lies. It was that they were clever lies, intricate lies, artful lies, lies delivered and maintained for months and years on end, lies that were perhaps not at the standard required for perjury but that were certainly far over the heads of the press itself. Even the greatest of them all, the finger-wagging 'I did not have sexual relations with that woman', was, in the end, a maddening matter of technical definition. And so it is now, with the furor over the pardon of Marc Rich. Is Clinton lying or not? Who knows?

The new crowd is different. The lies of Bush and his team, so far, are artless. They are transparent. They have a quality of guilelessness, of hour-to-hour inconsistency, that makes them almost endearing. Consider three examples.

First, on the tax cuts. Bush's campaign advisers cooked up a $1.6 trillion tax cut over a year ago. Its purpose was simple: to ward off the primary threat from Steve Forbes, the political representative of the anti-philanthropic ultra-rich. The economy was growing and surpluses loomed forever, so the tax cut was a long-term measure, including abolition of the estate tax in a sneak attack on universities, hospitals, and nonprofits. But now, the same tax cut has become a short-term anti-recession tool – in spite of the fact that the big money, ten years from now, would flow mainly to people whose spending will not increase at all, even then.

Second, the proposal to drill for oil in the Arctic National Wildlife Reserve is, and always has been of interest to oilmen and to the state of

Alaska. It was, and remains, irrelevant to our current energy issues. Yet now, Gale Norton tells us that this oil is needed to relieve the electricity crisis in California – an issue that did not exist when Bush first promised to open the ANWR. Carl Pope of the Sierra Club rightly called Norton's statement 'garbage' noting that California generates less than 1 percent of its electricity from oil.

And now, we see that Don Evans, the fund-raiser turned Commerce Secretary, has stripped the Census Bureau of final authority to decide whether to use statistical sampling to correct for under-voting – excuse me, *under-counting* – of minorities and poor people in the 2000 Census. We hear that the President believes 'actual enumeration' is the fairest way to count the American population. Funny. I do recall James A. Baker III in Florida, just a few months ago, solemnly intoning against the *actual enumeration* of ballots, and in favor of a *machine count* – which is of course only a badly biased way to obtain a sample.

Why do these people say such things? They are not stupid. Rather, it is in their nature. This administration is composed of a surface layer of corporate chieftains, and their staffs. These folk have a public relations view of the world – according to which a public statement need not last longer than a news cycle.

That being so, our new leaders don't worry about the difference between truth and falsehood. The important thing, for most of them, is to meet the need to have said something. The press reports what it is told. Part of the audience, out there in the larger public, will be bamboozled. Others will not be, but so what? Tomorrow is another day.

In the business world, the real work of getting things done does not depend on persuasion. These things depend on intimidation, discipline, and money. And so it is for Bush's team. The difference is that instead of mergers, acquisition, and competing for markets, the new game involves decapitating the Democrats and disenfranchising their voters. This, the new guys feel, they can achieve when they need to.

And the press, for its part, is very happy. They observe normal business practice – 'corporate cool' as David Broder described Dick Cheney. This is the way their own companies work; the journalists feel comfortable, at home. Political reporting takes on the coloration of the business pages; one does not report harshly on the press releases of important firms.

And so, the laziness of the new lies fits perfectly with the laziness of those who cover them. All are contented. For now.

(*The Texas Observer*, 16 March 2001)

Defending Democrats ... and Democracy

Forgive me if I do not join the applause for Michael Moore and his they-all-do-it defense of George Bush, prominently excerpted on these pages on April 12.

Moore doesn't mention it, but Federal regulations require drafting, publication, public comment, hearings. It's a process that takes many months. Bill Clinton did not just 'decide' on January 19, 2001 to do something about carpal tunnel syndrome, or arsenic in drinking water. The planning started years back. It was managed meticulously from the White House by John Podesta, Clinton's chief of staff. There was specific intent to time the final rules for the very end of Clinton's term, after the 2000 election, and after the adjournment of a hostile Republican Congress.

What's more, had Al Gore assumed the Presidency on January 20, 2001, the ergonomics standards and other good things for working people would have taken effect. They would be law today. And it remains true that one man, more than any other single person, prevented that outcome. That man is Moore's hero, Ralph Nader.

As it happens, I'm not personally hostile to Nader. Actually, I admire the man. Nader makes a serious and substantial critique of the Democratic Party. But his Presidential candidacy was a disaster. And the attempt to pretend otherwise is a delusion.

I worked on Capitol Hill during the early years of Ronald Reagan. I didn't like that Administration. But the government of George W. Bush is worse. Reagan at least won his elections, having campaigned on his own ideas. Bush's strategy is to confuse the issues and to conceal his actions. His is government by mendacity and subterfuge, well suited to the manner of his taking power.

And don't kid yourselves: it could get worse. The fate of the Republic hangs, so far, on one vote in the Senate. Should the Republicans win that body back in November, watch what will happen to what remains of environmental protection, judicial integrity, civil liberties, the national parks and reserves, and budgets for everything except military procurement. You don't think these things are important? Wait until they're completely gone.

Recent events in Venezuela showed well the attitude of this government toward democracy – and its shamelessness when caught out by genuine popular anger. At least the *New York Times*, which welcomed the coup at first, managed to utter a flannel-mouthed apology when it collapsed. Condoleezza Rice, on the other hand, had the gall to call on President Hugo Chavez to respect 'constitutional processes'. This, to a constitutionally elected President, from an administration that favors military tribunals!

Another lesson comes this week from France, where the dowdy but effective Socialist Prime Minister, Lionel Jospin – the man who brought French workers a 35-hour work week (can you imagine?) – was driven from the Presidential race by Jean-Marie Le Pen, France's Pat Buchanan.

How did it happen? Jospin was not unpopular. Polls actually showed that he might have won the Presidency had he made it to the second round. No. The reason was that the French left behaved without discipline – running a Green, a Communist, a Trotskyite, a left Gaullist, and god-knows-what-all against Jospin in the first round. The right, with fewer candidates, had a strategic advantage – and they used it.

Something similar could happen – again – to the Democrats in 2004. The Republicans know this play-book. In 2000, Buchanan ran the Reform Party into the ground, taking away an alternative for the far right, just as Nader was providing one for the progressive left. True, the combination wasn't quite enough to win the election for George W. Bush. But it did bring the result to within stealing range.

And that brings me back to the man who actually won the popular vote in 2000 – by one half million votes.

Al Gore ran a much-maligned campaign in 2000. Many of us did not like his style. But the underlying fact is that, without Perot and with Nader, Gore was running under far more difficult conditions than Clinton ever faced. And Gore, nevertheless, won the election – but for the disenfranchisement of thousands of Florida's black voters and the failure to count, in full, the ballots that were actually cast in that state.

Al Gore reappeared last week, on the Op-Ed page of the *New York Times*. Gore stated our problem directly: this is an Administration of and for . . . Big Oil. No surprise, except in the clarity and candor of the message, and in the lucid spelling out of the implications, from foreign policy to the environment.

Is Al Gore running again? It seems that he is. Does he have a moral right to another chance? Let me suggest that he does. Will he be a better candidate than Edwards, Kerry, Lieberman, and the others? I suspect he will. Can he win? He did it once. Will he make a better President than George Bush? Of course.

And beating George Bush, in 2002 and 2004, is not merely the highest political objective. It's the only one.

(*The Texas Observer*, 10 May 2002)

Tracking Down the Corporate Crooks

Bill Black and James Galbraith

President George W. Bush has reassured us that 'From the antitrust laws of the 19th century to the S&L reforms of recent times, America has tackled financial problems when they appeared.' But the Savings & Loan reforms came seven years and 150 billion taxpayer dollars late. Nor did that problem merely 'appear' It was created, by a deregulation bill in 1982, overseen at that time by the Vice President, the elder George Bush.

From 1981 to 1988, the Reagan/Bush administration covered up the S&L debacle. During that time, they forced reductions in S&L examiners and fought against the top federal regulator, Ed Gray, who sounded the alarm. Charles Keating, the felon who drove Lincoln Savings into the most expensive S&L failure in history ($3 billion) considered Vice President Bush an ally in his efforts to force Gray from office. Only after he was safely elected President did George Bush propose to reregulate the S&L industry in 1989.

Meanwhile, Neil Bush, private citizen, was getting a 'loan' from a business partner. The partner invested the loan for Neil with the agreement that if the investment succeeded Neil would get all the profits and repay the debt, but if it failed he would not have to repay. Neil knew that this same business partner was not creditworthy and yet was borrowing over $100 million from Silverado S&L, where Neil was a member of the Board. Neil did not warn Silverado that the borrower was not creditworthy. When Silverado failed, the Office of Thrift Supervision proposed a minor enforcement action against Neil, which the Bush administration then attempted to block.

George W. Bush, private citizen, emulated Neil. He became rich through a buyout of his interest in the Texas Rangers at a huge profit. How did he purchase that interest in the first place? He got a very large loan from a very friendly bank. How was the bank able to justify the loan? If at all, because the value of Bush's shares in Harken were held up by Harken's accounting fraud. Why was he on Harken's Board of Directors and also a well-paid consultant? Because his name was Bush. Why was he able to sell his Harken shares for a profit? Because Harken committed a financial fraud that hid real losses and created fictional income.

What was the nature of that fraud? It was a variant on the Enron and Lincoln Savings frauds. Harken insiders formed a entity which 'purchased' Harken's bad assets for a grossly excessive price. But Harken financed almost all of the sale. If the bad assets had stayed on the books, Harken would have had to report severe losses, threatening its survival and causing its stock values to plummet. George W. Bush tells us 'You need to look back on the directors' minutes' to find out whether he voted to approve this fraudulent sale. (The minutes are, however, not available.) Whether he did or didn't, George W. Bush is a wealthy man today because his business friends were willing to stoop to fraud to make him rich.

George W. Bush is in trouble, in part, because of his clumsy cover-ups of this fraud. Knowing of the severe problems at Harken, Bush sold around 200,000 shares of stock for around four dollars. (We do not know who purchased Bush's shares, but was it the ever-friendly Harvard Management Corporation, which had started buying Harken when Bush joined it and had, by 1990, become one of its largest holders?) He then failed to file required notice of these sales. When challenged on that point, he first claimed that the SEC 'lost' his filing. His second story was to blame the failure on Harken's lawyers. But that won't wash. Bush was selling his *own* stock, and was therefore *personally* responsible for filing the documents.

Bush claims to see nothing wrong about Harken's frauds. 'There was an honest difference of opinion as to how to account for a complicated transaction.' 'Sometimes things aren't exactly black and white when it comes to accounting procedures.' Both comments are misleading. The sole purpose of the transaction was fraudulent. The goal was to hide real losses and to book fictional income. The people who made the decision and the board of directors who approved it stood to gain directly from the fraud, and Bush did benefit – enormously.

Bush is also wrong on the accounting. This was a *deliberately* complicated transaction for the same reason that Enron's and Lincoln Savings' partnerships were complicated. The people who design frauds know that complexity makes it hard for regulators to discern them.

While the transaction was complicated, the underlying fraud is so well known that the accounting rules governing such transactions are *not* vague. There was no 'honest dispute' about accounting rules. There was a deliberate fraud *structured* in a complicated manner in order to be able to claim that it wasn't really deliberate.

Now, Bush tells us that the Securities and Exchange Commission needs to be strengthened. But he appointed an SEC head, Harvey Pitt, who as a lawyer for the accountants led the campaign to block the Clinton Administration's effort to clean up the accounting profession. Pitt promptly *cut* the SEC staff and killed the SEC initiatives to clean up accounting. Back in Texas, then-Governor Bush was proud that he had made it extremely difficult for securities fraud victims to receive compensation through lawsuits. When the Enron scandal broke, Bush continued this line, suggesting that *victims* of fraud who bring suits are 'extort[ionists]'. He, and Republicans in the House, have fought vigorously to stop real accounting reform.

President George W. Bush is right to bring up the S&L debacle as an analogy. He is following in his father's footsteps: first, create the problem by taking actions that encourage fraud. Second, do nothing while the frauds become epidemic. And finally, when the scandal breaks, claim like Claude Rains in *Casablanca* that he is 'shocked, *shocked*' that gambling is going on. In Mr Bush's case, the winnings from that gambling were safely pocketed long ago.

Note

Bill Black and James Galbraith teach at the University of Texas at Austin. Black, a lawyer and criminologist, was counsel to the Federal Home Loan Bank Board in the early 1980s; Galbraith is an economist.

(*Boston Globe*, 23 July 2002)

The Realities of Resistance

The voters have spoken – the bastards!

(Morris Udall)

So George W. Bush has won a national election. He did it by an astounding mixture of war fever, money, and media manipulation. But that is beside the point. From now on, his presidency will carry weight that for many of us it did not carry before.

The Democrats are a party of failure and disappointment. Dick Gephardt, an honorable man, played his hand correctly after September 11, 2001 by lining up behind Bush at that time. But the decision to do the same over Iraq was wrong, in principle and also in political terms. Tom Daschle, an able leader, has proved that one cannot lead both a divided caucus and a national opposition.

And so, amazingly, in the last days the Democratic message became . . . nostalgia for Bill Clinton. But Clinton's interventions in Florida, North Carolina and Massachusetts had no effect, except possibly to mobilize Republican voters. Clearly, they loathe Clinton, and even Democrats who like him do not want him back. We now know that Al Gore was plainly right in his decision not to use Clinton in the campaign two years ago.

The Senate is Republican again. Judgeships and eventually Supreme Court nominees will now go through. The estate tax will be repealed for good; over time America's social landscape will be transformed. We will see a massive new tax cut for business, very soon. Later on, the resulting deficits will be used to try to force the privatization of Social Security.

Against this, the Democratic Party must become again a party that speaks plainly for health care, the minimum and the living wage, for revenue sharing to save states and local government from collapse, for Social Security and for the public schools. These priorities must come far above tax cuts and the useless desire to balance the budget. The

18

Democrats must be a party plainly against empire, against the pluto-
crats and the corporate crooks and the zombie judges and tax levelers.
A party that speaks and fights for women and minorities and immigrants and working families. A party that fights for civil and political
and workers' rights and for the environment.

This has not happened yet. My tireless correspondent Roger Baker
explains why not:

> If the Dems move to the left and tell the truth, then their corporate
> cash evaporates. If they move to the right to get more cash, they
> become quasi-Republicans, but remain less appealing than the real
> thing. An impossible paradox that will be resolved only by a ripen-
> ing economic crisis.

But there is a way out. We know now that cash, bereft of message,
cannot beat the Republicans. We know from the 2000 election
that a fighting populism can. We should know too that third parties
offer no way out – the American public is not going to turn Green.

But the economic crisis will surely ripen in the months ahead. It will
deepen needs and grievances that were mostly absent two years ago
and that are still not very widespread today. While the Republicans
will move swiftly to stimulate economic growth, with tax cuts and low
interest rates, it is not a given that they will succeed.

Who, then, is to lead? The answer must be: the person who steps
forward, like Charles de Gaulle in London, to organize the resistance.
The next Democratic leader will be the one who forges, from this
defeat, an opposition party. The Dick Gephardt of old, Ted Kennedy,
Paul Wellstone – they are the models that we need now. Only from a
resistance can a leader emerge.

Could it be Al Gore? Gore's presumptive right to a rematch has now
vanished. He must now earn his role as a leader from the ground up.
And having broken eloquently with Bush over Iraq, he must also now
break with Clinton, whose economics of tight budgets and easy money
cannot be reproduced any more. Conditions have changed; Gore needs
his own plan. Whether he has the stamina, the drive, the intensity –
and most of all the vision – to produce an effective one is for him to
prove, in the battles about to unfold.

In this moment of defeat, the resistance is undefined. Leadership is
up for grabs. It could be someone old. It could be someone new. But
someone must step forward, and begin to organize, if the Democratic
Party is to survive. There is no alternative, sorry to say, and despicable

though our collective performance in the 2002 elections may have been.

(*The Texas Observer*, 22 November 2002)

Why Bush Likes a Bad Economy

Almost nine million people are unemployed. Many millions more are underemployed, and most of all, underpaid. Millions more lack health insurance. States are cutting basic public services everywhere, while the taxes – property and sales, mainly – to pay for those that remain are rising. And the gates of opportunity – for instance, to attend college – are closing on millions more.

George Bush did not entirely create this problem. The bubble and the bust of high technology, the obsession with a strong dollar, the debt build-up of American households – these existed before we got George Bush. The late 1990s were a moment of prosperity and that rarest of economic achievements – full employment. But the boom was based on dreams, illusions, and mortgages. These set the stage for a slump that began in late 2000, from which we have not recovered and will not recover soon.

But Bush has done nothing to make our economic problem better and much to make it worse. We have lost more than two million jobs since he took office, and almost half a million just since the 2002 election. In the face of this, the bulk of the Bush tax cuts went, notoriously, to the very wealthy, whose spending is little affected. Many middle-class Americans face tax increases – in property and sales taxes at the state and local level. And meanwhile, Bush is bent on eroding pay and working conditions, with the most recent outrage being the assault on fair labor standards affecting overtime. As for the minimum wage? Forget about it.

In the near term, it is true that new tax cuts and more military spending may bring another false dawn. The second quarter GDP growth of 2.4 percent was a sign of this. Meanwhile Federal Reserve Chairman Alan Greenspan is doing his best to keep the housing bubble aloft. Greenspan knows about blowing bubbles, but not even he can forever prevent them from popping. Short-term fiscal expansion and continued low interest rates may prevent an early renewal of recession. They will not, however, bring us back to full employment.

The reason for this lies in the financial position of the private sector. American households in the late 1990s embarked on an unprecedented period of sustained spending above their incomes, financed by borrowing that was supported by rising home equity and the stock bubble. This was a remarkable event. For fifty years following World War II, Americans had always spent a little less than they earned. Never before on record here – and rarely anywhere – did an entire population go into a position of dissaving. But it happened. And it could not last.

The collapse of stocks in 2000 started an effort to get consumption and incomes back into line by cutting the growth rate of spending. But the continuing reduction of interest rates has kept that adjustment from completing. The potential therefore remains for a substantial future deceleration in household spending, something that would be much aggravated if interest rates go up. Since household spending is well over 60 percent of national expenditures, the further depressing effect of this, when it eventually occurs, will be substantial. It hasn't happened yet, but that doesn't mean that it won't.

The other big problem going forward is our very weak position in foreign trade. We have a propensity, now deeply entrenched, to run huge foreign deficits at full employment. Given that propensity, the economy needs a huge net stimulus to reach full employment in the first place. In the late 1990s, the impulse came from the tech boom and the willingness of households to borrow. But the investment boom is over, and the debt-capacity of households seems to be nearing exhaustion. Even the mortgage-refinancing boom, brought on by successive cuts in interest rates, is now evidently nearing an end.

So long as households, businesses and also state and local governments are still retrenching, one of two things must happen to support a sustained expansion and return to full employment. Either federal budget deficits must rise by a phenomenal further amount, or the United States must find a way to increase exports and reduce imports relative to GDP, thus making it possible for a smaller budget deficit to do the job on domestic employment.

If a budget deficit double its current size is unfathomable and the trade regime inviolate (as one must suppose, for political reasons), then the implication is plain. We face a long period of economic stagnation, in which a return to full employment cannot be obtained – until the household and business sectors make a full financial adjustment on their own. For that, we would have to wait.

Can the falling dollar square this circle, giving us lower foreign deficits and so reducing the need for fiscal expansion? This appears unlikely. On one side, estimates of the price elasticity of American exports suggest that a lower dollar will not increase foreign demand for American products by leaps and bounds. On the other side, the imports of US consumer goods come substantially from countries (such as Mexico and China) against whose currencies the dollar has not declined, and who are prepared to suffer considerable hardship to prevent such a decline in order to maintain their present access to the US market. Therefore these imports are not becoming markedly more expensive, and the demand for them is unlikely to be choked off by considerations of cost. Things could change on their own: American households might tire of cheap clothing, fancy athletic shoes, and electronic toys. But given how much these items contribute to the modest comforts of American life, this also seems very unlikely.

Finally, one may doubt the willingness of the Treasury and Federal Reserve to tolerate a declining dollar – even one that is falling only against the euro – for an indefinite period. At some point, speculators will kick in, considerations of national pride will be raised, some Latin American debtors may default, and US banks may begin to object to the erosion of their international position. A dollar defense, effected by raising interest rates, could quickly throw the internal economy into deep recession.

The baseline outlook then, is not one where a return to full employment prosperity might be achieved by modest changes in policy. A little 'stimulus' – pushing a few well-chosen buttons in the tax code – will not do it. Nor can Greenspan be counted on; the Federal Reserve has largely run out of tricks. An Administration committed to changing this situation will have to be prepared with strong measures.

No such measures are coming from George Bush. The men in charge under Bush talk about growth, of course. One might think that they must be disappointed by this dilemma if they understand it. They do, after all, face an election next year.

But in fact, we are seeing an interesting departure from the normal pattern of Republican election-year populism. Richard Nixon in 1972 and Ronald Reagan in 1984 ran strong-growth policies that reduced unemployment and produced whopping election margins. (Nixon even imposed price-wage controls, which drove real wages through the roof.) Under Bush – despite the seemingly large fiscal deficits brought about by recession, tax cuts, and war – the expansionary impetus is weaker. And the Administration is making no concessions in its war on labor rights.

Why not? It may be that economic stagnation is to their taste. They don't want a new recession, obviously, and they look set to avoid that. But do they really want full employment and strong labor unions and rising wages? Probably not. The oil, mining, defense, media, and pharmaceutical firms who form the core of their constituency rely on monopoly power, patents, and the control of public resources for their profits. They do not depend, very much, on strong consumer demand.

As for the election, there are no Bush Democrats. The Nixon Democrats in the South long ago turned Republican, while the Reagan Democrats up North seem to have largely returned to the fold. (Michigan, for instance, went comfortably for Gore.) In a weaker economy, too, it may be that turnout will decline, helping Bush. The calculation is therefore plain. A strong economy won't help that much, and a weak economy won't hurt that much, either. And if it does, the effect can be drowned in a sea of grateful campaign money – or by some new national security crisis.

Stagnation, moreover, helps to justify more tax cuts. The Administration's core policy objective in this area is to shield financial wealth from all taxation. Two years ago, estate and income taxes were cut. This year it was capital gains, dividends, and again the top tax rate. Next year the sunset provisions in these measures will be removed. As things are going, quite soon, taxes will fall mainly on real estate, payrolls, and consumption. This is to say that taxes will be paid mostly by the middle class, by the working class, and by the poor. That is what the Administration wants, and what – if not defeated – it is exceedingly likely to get.

Finally, stagnation and the Bush tax policy promote right-wing plans to cut and privatize essential services, including health, education, and pensions. As financial wealth escapes tax, neither states, nor cities, nor the federal government can provide vital services – except by taxing sales and property at rates that will provoke tax rebellions, especially when middle-class incomes are not rising. Every public service will fall between the hammer of tax cuts and the anvil of deficits in state, local, and federal budgets. The streets will be dirtier, as also the air and the water. Emergency rooms will back up even more than they have; more doctors will refuse public patients. More fire houses and swimming pools and libraries will be closed. Public universities will cost more; the public schools will lose the middle class. Eventually federal budget deficits will collide with Social Security and Medicare, putting privatization back on the agenda.

I am from Texas, where you can see this future happening now.

Say what you will, the Bush team is plainly not pandering after votes. They are pursuing a governing agenda that favors the factions they represent: tax cuts for the misanthropic wealthy; tax increases for the middle class; imperial control over oil; deregulation, privatization, and cuts in public services at all levels; defiance of international agreements; a systematic spoilage of the environment; an all-out offensive against labor rights; and the placement of right-wingers in government, most insidiously in the courts.

In the face of this reality, full economic recovery is going to be hard, even if a Democrat wins the next election. It cannot be done, certainly, by a simple return to policies of the Clinton era. Nor can it be done by stimulus alone – a simple matter of spending more and finding the right taxes to cut. We will need to rewrite – once again – the tax code. We will need a revenue-sharing program to stabilize the states and cities. We will need to re-establish the rule of law in the corporate world. We will need to help labor reset minimum fair standards. We will need a new energy and environmental strategy consistent with geophysical realities and the dangers of, among other things, climate change, and including, as we've just learned, a public initiative to re-regulate power and rebuild the electricity grid. We will need a new international financial structure and possibly a new trade regime. Along the way, there will be the hard economic challenge of overcoming the financial obstacles left over from the late 1990s – compounded as they are by the indifference and corruption of the Bush gang.

It would be good if the Democrats were to begin, fairly soon, to think seriously about these issues. It is of course possible that Bush has miscalculated. The election next year may turn out to matter after all. If so, some poor Democrat could end up in very deep trouble, come January 2005.

(*The Progressive*, October 2003)

The No-Jobs President

The transcendent economic issue isn't the growth rate. It isn't the stock market. It isn't the budget deficit. And it isn't even the rate of unemployment. It's number of people in this country who have decent work.

Here's a chart, taken almost directly from the Bureau of Labor Statistics. It shows the month-to-month change in total employment,[1] and how it fell from an average gain of 236,000 during the Clinton Presidency to an average loss of 66,000 per month under George Bush. The arrow, which I added, shows when Bush took office. Economic numbers don't get clearer than this.

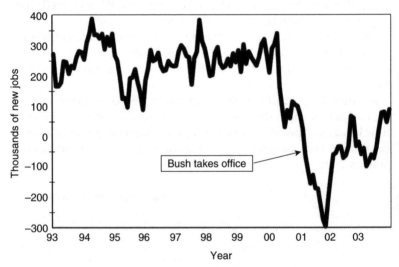

Figure 1   Employment (monthly change, 1993–2003)

Next, notice when the deep dive ends. That's right: it was just *after* September 11, 2001. It's true Bush ought not to be blamed for the job losses of the Internet bust. But neither can he properly blame *his* troubles on Osama Bin Laden. Job losses slowed down when the War on Terror began.

Bush should be judged on the record after that – on the creation of jobs in 2002 and 2003. After all, the recession officially ended in November 2001. How many new jobs did we get since then? An average *loss* of 22,000 jobs every month.

There are no new jobs. Total job growth in the Clinton years: 23 million. Total job *losses* so far in the Bush years: over two million. Total gains in the last six months, since the so-called recovery supposedly accelerated in the third quarter? Just 221,000. That's less than a single month's average under Clinton. And last month? One thousand new jobs.

How many jobs *should* there have been? Crudely, the Clinton pace over three years would have yielded about 8.5 million. Allowing Bush a pass for 2001, matching Clinton in just two years would have meant 5.6 million new jobs, not the loss of another half a million. Want more? Lee Price of the Economic Policy Institute has a very useful study.[2]

Bush's minions whitewash these figures by pointing to the household employment survey, which shows more (though not great) job growth. Here's the main difference: the household survey covers 60,000 households. The payroll survey covers 400,000 *businesses* (and millions of workers). The payroll survey measures real jobs. Most agree that the payroll survey, while not perfect (it misses some new jobs in the upswing), is the better of the two.

The household survey does pick up many people who call themselves self-employed, independent contractors and the like. (When academics do this, we call it 'consulting'.) Some would have you believe that this is the future of the economy, but let's hope not. Most such work is stop-gap, a way to scrape by when regular work is hard to find. Most people doing it would abandon it for a real job, if they could, in a minute. Real jobs are better.

True, the unemployment *rate* doesn't look so bad. But why not? Partly because many people who can't get unemployment insurance now get themselves on the disabled rolls if they can. (Disability, the refuge of the desperate, has been growing very fast.) And the jobless rate did fall in December. But why? Because many thousands of people stopped looking for work. Some retired. A few went back to school.

Most just went home to wait it out. Very sensible of them, under these conditions.

The Bush years are a study in *deliberately* wasted effort. Repeal of the estate tax. Tax exemption for stock dividends. Ballistic Missile Defense. The Patriot Act. The war on Iraq. Each of these initiatives has a clientele. None of them seriously aims to achieve its stated goal, be that economic recovery or homeland security or national security writ large.

The method is clear to any who choose to study closely. It is a method of subterfuge and deception. It is the systematic and relentless pursuit of partly-hidden agendas, sold to the public with slogans. The tax cuts were not aimed to produce recovery and jobs: they were a reward to the rich. The war on Iraq was not waged to help the war on terror: it was about getting Saddam, as Paul O'Neill has now confirmed. Missile defense is not about North Korea, still less about Iran or any other 'rogue state': it's about the contracts. In all these cases, the decision on what to do came first. And then the circumstances of the day were arranged to suit.

So it is today on the economy. What does Bush want? He wants a growth rate high enough to get him through the election. That's obvious. After that, he doesn't care. His clientele – the military contractors, oil companies, pharmaceutical firms and big media that control this government – make their money on patents, contracts, and the exercise of monopoly power. (Case in point: Bush is pressuring impoverished Central Americans, in trade negotiations, to add *ten years* to the length of *drug patents*.) These people have no interest in full employment. They like unemployment, weak labor, low wages, and a government that bullies on their behalf. And after the election, if Bush wins, that is what they will get, for four more years.

Bush has levers for 2004. Child care credits kicked in during the third quarter of 2003. Households spent them at once, hence the 8 percent annualized growth rate that mesmerized the country for a moment. Tax refunds are due in the next few months; that should give spending another kick. The cost of war was the first big push that the economy got last year. Now much military equipment needs replacing; spending on that may be felt soon.

Most important, monetary policy is toeing Bush's line. Alan Greenspan and his deputies were all over the economists' meetings in San Diego this month, promising that interest rates will stay down. Don't misunderstand me: this is the right policy. But for how long will it last? Low interest rates imperil the global dollar. The pressure to defend the dollar is out there. Will it prevail once the election is past? Remember: after November George Bush will not care.

And after the election, the stagnation they want will not be hard to achieve. Our economy still faces major barriers to sustained growth. Capacity utilization in industry is low: a barrier to sustained growth of investment. Household debt burdens are high: a barrier to accelerating consumer spending, which will be aggravated when the housing bubble eventually pops. Federal, state and local budgets are riddled with structural deficits; these will not go away with growth. In the states and localities, spending cuts and tax increases are the only agenda. At the federal level, the deficit hawks – a well-meaning group, but prone to obsess on the wrong issue – will be on the march next year.

In short, the most likely outlook is for strong growth in the first half of the year, and stagnation thereafter. Businesses know this. So they will ramp up production to meet demand, but remain resolutely reluctant to hire new workers for the long term. The bad jobs picture is more than just a sign of the failure of trickle-down. It is a measure of the lack of confidence that ordinary American business has in the long-term future. Businesses in America are hard to fool, and they are not expecting another long boom.

The election, in short, will be a race between the campaign propaganda of growth rates and the realities of scarce jobs, low pay, and stagnant living standards. But reality has a way of holding its own in people's minds. It's not yet clear, by any means, that truth won't prevail.

And so now comes George Bush, with two more great proposals to get the country moving again. The first is immigration 'reform', ginned up just before a big summit in Monterrey, Mexico to play to the Hispanic vote. The proposal promises minor conveniences to the estimated eight million undocumented workers in this country.

But at what price?

The new class of migrants would have to leave when their permits are up, unless renewed. They would have to leave if fired from their jobs. In a word, employers would judge who stays in the country and who is kicked out. Forget labor rights. Forget unions. Also forget family, home, neighborhood, things like that. Anyone wanting to protect those things will stay out of sight.

Worse, workers coming into the program would in practice be giving up their path to political rights. They would, for the most part, never become citizens. They would never get to vote. No one will represent their interests. No one will speak for their schools, their clinics, their wages. No one will stand in their defense when they are abused on the job, hurt, sacked, blacklisted, and sent home.

There is worse still. Bush made clear that this program is not just for workers presently in the country, as the press has mostly been reporting. It is not just for those who may soon arrive. No, it is far broader than that. Here's the President's speech:

> If an American employer is offering a job that American citizens are not willing to take, we ought to welcome into our country a person who will fill that job.

This program will permit any employer to admit any worker. From any country. At any time. The only requirement is that it be for a job Americans are *not* willing to take. But it is easy to create such jobs. Cut wages. Terminate the unions. Lengthen the hours. Speed up the lines. Chicken farmers have known this for years. Bush's plan is a blank check for every bad boss this country has.

There is no reason why principal recruitment of new workers would be from Mexico. It might be, very massively, from China. Or perhaps from India, with its large English-speaking population. Temp agencies would go out on recruiting missions. Some of this competition may displace Mexican and Central American nationals presently working illegally in the United States (and hoping to stay). That would only drive them even further underground.

And for those who take up the program, register as temporary workers, and then see their permits expire? Bush is at pains to say that he expects this group to go home. But who will make them? Will the government organize a mass campaign of roundups and deportations? Or will the workers just quietly disappear back into the sub-underground of the truly illegal?

And for those who do go home, who will replace them? Another cohort of strangers? This is a program to create a *rotating* underclass of foreign workers, who never assimilate to American ways or adopt American values. It's hard to imagine anything worse for our social life – or for that matter for our national security.

For millions of *citizen* workers, what would happen? The answer is clear. Bad bosses drive out the good. Good bosses will turn bad under pressure. The terms of our jobs would get worse and worse. Who would want *a citizen worker*? A *bracero* will be so much cheaper, more loyal, and under control. And who among us, in our right mind, would want to look for work? Unless, of course, we needed to eat. Or pay the mortgage. I am not exaggerating: this is a threat to us all.

What indeed, would be left for citizens to do? Perhaps they will get first call on that other great Bush idea, the moon base and mission to Mars. Here we see the hand of Bush's space science adviser, Karl ('Spirit') Rove(r). NASA, you may have noticed, has just sent a mission to Mars. It was cheap as these things go, safe – and spectacular. Rove would take that money and put it into sending up a human: dumb, dangerous, and expensive. But I'd be for it, if we could send *him* on the mission. And his boss.

Note

1. Payroll jobs, averaged over three months to make the chart easier to read.
2. At http://www.epinet.org/content.cfm/briefingpapers_bp146.

(*Salon*, 19 January 2004)

Bush's Hail Mary

George W. Bush has held office for 36 months. How is he doing politically, and what can we learn from a detached look at the record?

Here's a chart of Bush's job approval rating, as reported by the entire panoply of pollsters – Newsweek, Fox, ABC-Washington Post, Zogby, CNN-Time, CBS-New York Times, Gallup-CNN, NBC-Wall Street Journal, and Pew – all thoughtfully collected by PollingReport.com.

First of all, notice how closely the polls track. True, the ABC-Washington Post poll tends to run a little high. Pew and Zogby tend to

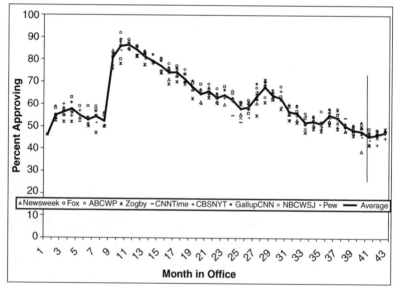

Figure 2 Bush job approval

run a little low. But the range is not large, and all of the polls move in the same direction at the same time. This suggests they are measuring something real. The pollsters may be redundant, but they have not been wasting their time.

What is the message of these numbers? One stands out: in his entire first term, only three episodes so far have gained approval for Bush. All were related to terrorism and to war. They were 9/11, the war on Iraq, and the capture of Saddam. Taken together, the five months when Bush gained popularity on these events account for 89 percent of all the variation in the change of Bush's job approval, measured by the average of these polls.

It is not surprising that Bush's State of the Union speech dwelt so heavily on war and terror.

But equally, consider what has happened in the other 32 months. The record is remarkably consistent: in the range of approvals above 48 percent or so – that is, among voters who did not vote for him in 2000 – Bush loses support, month after month. And he does so at what is nearly a constant rate. Tick, tock.

Measured by a number of different techniques (including regression analysis), Bush's monthly loss of approval appears to be a little less than 1.6 percentage points – every month, on average. And the variation around that average (standard error) is quite small: less than one-fourth of that value. That means that in 95 percent of the cases, the decline is between 0.9 and 2.3 percent per month. Tick, tock.

It seems that Bush has done nothing to win the enduring allegiance of voters who did not already support him in 2000. After each rallying event, some give up immediately. Others take longer. But the trend is consistent: gains accrued in crisis decay over time.

One might say that this is a judgment about character, a perception of who Bush is and what interests he serves. But it does not seem to matter what Bush says or does. Also, so far – though of course this could change – no effect from better economic news can be found. Tick, tock.

We cannot say that the erosion will continue as Bush's approval slips into 'red' territory – below the 48 percent or so who supported him to begin with. Indeed, there is no evidence that Bush's Republican base has eroded at all. What we can infer, reasonably, is that there is a strong tendency in the electorate to revert, over time, to the sharp and narrow division of the last election. Tick, tock.

The numbers tell us one other thing: 9/11 was worth 36 points of approval over two months. The Iraq war was worth a bit over 12 points, again over two months. The capture of Saddam was worth five points in one month. In each case, we add the actual gain to the 1.6 points Bush would have otherwise lost, to read out the difference that the particular event made.

So, let's assume (favorably for Bush) that Bush's approval slide stops entirely at 48 percent. How much of a boost will he need to achieve a safe 53 percent or so by election day?

Clearly, another 9/11, arriving anytime this year, would guarantee the election. But 9/11, let us hope, was a one-time event. It is not obvious that a second attack, on a similar or even a larger scale, would have the same political effect. It might turn into a political disaster. In any event, let us suppose that the manufacture of such an atrocity is safely beyond the pale.

Theoretically, another war is within the administration's power to wage or not to wage. There are well-known targets: Syria and North Korea. If a war against either one were launched in August, then on the Iraqi model Bush would be up about 10 points in November.

But a second war seems remote just now. Unlike Iraq, North Korea may well have the bomb – an authentic deterrent. Unlike Iraq, Syria is not seriously thought by anyone to pose a threat to the United States. The propaganda buildup isn't there; the weapons-of-mass-destruction trick will not work twice. Bush would have no allies on such a mission; it is impossible to imagine UN support. And US military forces remain more heavily stretched by the Iraqi occupation than the war planners hoped they would be. Even if they were nearly out by June – which is doubtful – it is hard to imagine their being ready to fight again in August.

What if on the other hand there is peace: an Iraqi government in place and our troops come home, safe and sound, over the summer? That could happen, and it might help Bush out. But the timing is delicate. Do it too early and the effect will wear off by October. Do it too late and the risk is that the fedayeen or the Shiites will spoil the endgame.

So what does that leave? Another Saddam. And, of course, he is conveniently out there. If the capture of Osama bin Laden is worth the same as the capture of Saddam, the answer to Bush's electoral dilemma is plain: get Osama in October.

Like all statistical analyses, this one is no better than its assumptions. We have assumed that Bush will bottom out at 48 percent, other things being equal. We assume there are no dramatic new events – such as a war not of our own making, or (say) an assassination attempt against Bush or his challenger. We assume that Osama, even after three years of hiding out (presumably in Pakistan), will be worth as much as Saddam. Of course, if Al Qaeda hits us again this year, he might be worth more.

That leaves one question: what price would Bush have to pay – and to whom – in order to bring him in, just in the nick of time?

(*Salon*, 9 February 2004)

The Plutocrats Go Wild

Next year's economic difficulties are already on the horizon. Growth is slowing, as the housing market cools and consumers rein in their spending. Inflation is rising a bit, driven mainly by oil prices, health care costs, and corporate price increases fueling a spectacular recent profit surge. Job creation is weak and wages are flat. This is the New Stagflation – an unpleasant reminder of the economic cost of unilateral war.

But George W. Bush has never tried to fix the economy in the short term. His focus is on making long-term – and, he hopes, irreversible – changes: to taxes and social programs, to foreign policy, and to the government's capacity to regulate the environment, natural resource use, and corporate behavior.

Bush's top economic priority has always been to cut taxes on the wealthy; as he famously said, the 'have-mores' are his political base. The marginal income tax rate, the estate tax, the tax on dividends, and the proceeds of the profits tax all fell sharply in his first term. His second term could finish the job, shifting the tax base to consumption, perhaps even abolishing the income tax for a value-added tax (as Speaker Dennis Hastert now suggests). Virtually the whole tax burden will then fall on the middle class, on working Americans and on the poor.

As revenues fall, spending programs will come under new attack. Not defense spending, of course: the Pentagon will remain inviolate. Indeed the military may demand still more spending, as the true costs of pacifying Iraq gradually become clear. New arms races – with North Korea over missiles and missile defense – and new conflicts, perhaps with Iran or China, may come into view. We will need many more soldiers, and much more money, if such conflicts occur.

And so, given the budget deficits ahead, the battle royal will be fought over what remains of federal social spending. With Alan Greenspan at his side, Bush will challenge Congress to slice, dice, and eviscerate. The privatization of Social Security – an invisible issue right now – will surely resurface once the votes are safely cast in November.

Meanwhile Greenspan will try to steer between a cost-driven price inflation and a sagging labor market. Should he raise interest rates or hold the line? The Fed started boosting rates just before the recent spate of bad economic news: slower growth, weak job gains, slumping consumer spending, falling producer prices. This shows that its insight into our present problems isn't deep.

Indeed the Fed is driving blind. Greenspan is aiming for a 'natural interest rate', whose value, as he admits, he doesn't know. How this idea came to dominate Fed thinking isn't clear: the concept is a throwback to the economics of a century ago, and is the basis of almost no modern research. But we do know that higher interest rates will mean more pressure on debt-ridden households, slower consumer spending growth, and stagnant or falling stock prices – as anyone can see.

Bush's second term may see a crisis of the dollar, now heavily reliant on reserve-asset stockpiling by China and Japan, who own a huge amount of our debt paper. In effect, those countries are sending us cheap goods in return for expensive paper, working hard for no current material reward. Will they continue this odd behavior for four more years, even if tensions erupt over Korea or Taiwan? Or will China, especially, diversify into euros, or perhaps into commodities, aggravating global inflation? Will the neglected states of Latin America, increasingly alienated from the United States, set off a banking crisis with debt defaults? We'll see. The dangers are real, and we are totally unprepared.

All of this exactly brings to mind the late nineteenth century, a time of budding empires, rapacious trusts, Social Darwinism and populist upheaval. Plutocracy and consumption taxes, wars of conquest, chronic unemployment and rising poverty, a world economy dominated by financial panics and the commodity cycle – these formed the economic scene. George Bush and his allies have been modeling themselves on William McKinley – the champion of vested interests in the Gilded Age.

Fortunately for America, McKinley was succeeded by Teddy Roosevelt, a progressive Republican who fought the monopolies and favored the environment, and then by Woodrow Wilson, a Democrat who got us the income tax and inspired the search for a global system of collective security. True, it took another generation to break finally with rule by the corporate rich. But eventually there did come the Great Depression and Franklin Roosevelt, who gave us public works, Social Security, the National Labor Relations Act, the SEC and the UN.

The cozy plutocracy of McKinley and his successors – Taft, Harding, Coolidge, Hoover – could not stand before the needs of the modern world. It can't be brought back now. Bush's effort to do so will bring misery for many, perhaps for many years. But the final outcome is not in doubt. Bush's second term will fail, and America will change course; democracy and common sense will assert themselves in the end.

(*The Washington Monthly*, September 2004)

Dissecting Cheney

The final verdict of history may dismiss George W. Bush as a front man who was not quite up to his job. But nothing like that will be said of Dick Cheney. Cheney is undeniably intelligent, powerful, and shrewd – a force to be reckoned with, even though operating mainly in the shadows.

The key to Cheney is that he is a throwback, to a brand of strategic thinking that bedeviled the Cold War. He is part of the legacy that runs back to Generals Curtis LeMay and Thomas Power of the Strategic Air Command in the late 1950s. The two tenets of this legacy are absolutely consistent: (1) overestimate the enemy and govern through fear, and (2) hit them before they can hit you. The Missile Gap and the First Strike, in four words.

Cheney's school never quite seized control of American strategic policy while the Soviet Union existed. It came close on several occasions, including the Cuban missile crisis. It often won budget and political battles through trickery, such as the CIA Team B exercise of the early 1980s, which led to Missile Defense. But the first strike never happened. In the end cooler and wiser heads, from Eisenhower, Kennedy and Johnson through Nixon and Reagan, always saw the advantages of working with Soviet leaders to prevent war.

Economic competition with the Soviet bloc had the logic of warfare. The Soviet Union and its empire represented an alternative industrial system, capable of absorbing the world's oil, gold, uranium and other strategic resources. Denying them access to key supplies – oil in the Middle East, gold in South Africa, uranium in Zaire and elsewhere – was the cornerstone of covert strategy in those years, dictating many ugly political choices. This too formed Dick Cheney. It helps explain why, as late as 1986, he opposed a congressional resolution pressing for the release of Nelson Mandela from his South African prison.

The larger economic balance of the Cold War was a third element in Cheney's upbringing. With the non-communist industrial world, the United States cut a simple bargain. We provided security – including naval control of the oceans and a nuclear umbrella over Europe and Japan. They in turn tolerated a dollar-based world financial system, permitting the United States to live far above its productive powers. America's perpetual trade deficits were balanced, in simple terms, by the bomb and the fleet.

Ten years after the Soviet Union collapsed, the shadowy hard men of the Cold War finally came into uncontested power in the United States. And to our tragic cost, they brought unchanged thinking to a radically different world. Their solution? To recreate in the minds of the public a world that would resemble, as much as possible, the dangerous but politically familiar one in which they had been formed.

Before September 11, 2001, Bush and Cheney searched for an enemy that could generate an appropriate level of fear. North Korea was an early candidate; Bush in his first days cut off the South Korean Sunshine Initiative and used the supposed North Korean missile threat as the prime lever behind Cheney's key military priority at that time, Missile Defense. Reality however intruded: Kim Jong-Il could not fill Stalin's shoes. So China got a try-out too – lots of early tub-thumping about a supposedly growing threat to Taiwan. But then came the EP-3 incident, when a Navy spy plane was forced to land on Hainan Island, and the Chinese interned the crew and dissected the aircraft, which they eventually returned, disassembled and packed in boxes. This seems to have persuaded Team Bush that Team China was apt to make them look like fools.

September 11, 2001 put all of this into the background. But though the Global War on Terror was rooted in a real event, it was conducted in a way fundamentally oriented to the political opportunities it created, not to the actual dangers it revealed. Thus the neglect of port security, the squeeze on first responders, the negligence at Tora Bora, the flippant attitude toward the nuclear risks in the Russian stockpiles and the Pakistani labs. Thus the pathetic system of colored alerts, and the round-ups and detentions of irrelevant people, not a single one of whom has been convicted of a terrorism-related offense in the three years since.

Rule through fear remains an essential part of Cheney's message; he reiterates it every day on the stump. But three years after September 11, the message no longer resonates. It has come to sound, to most Americans, like an excuse for failure in every other sphere.

And overseas, the Clash of Civilizations has never worked as a cry for the mobilization of the West. The major European states are not conned, and neither is Japan. They have much more experience of political terror than we do – and they realize that the real job of rolling up the terror networks is, for the most part, a national and international police problem. For this reason, the global bargain that held up the dollar through the Cold War is imperilled. You can be sure, Cheney has no idea how to restore it.

Cheney's actual conduct in Iraq recaptures almost exactly the two operational doctrines of the Shadow Cold War. It is now obvious that his strategic vision centers on physical control of the world's oil. And his justification of the attack on Iraq, delivered on August 26, 2002, was a pure statement of the hidden doctrine of the First Strike.

Oil maps of Iraq and lists of foreign companies doing business there were found in the archives of Cheney's Energy Task Force. What does this prove? First, that the Task Force was not solely concerned with domestic energy policy and regulation, as it was said to be. It was, at least in part, a forum for considering the control of global oil. At worst, the map and list constitute evidence that the conquest of Iraq was on the corporate agenda from the beginning of the Bush years.

But why? What advantage do we, the United States, get from boots on the ground in the oil fields? It may seem a naive question, but it is not.

It is theoretically possible that we did it purely for corporate gain. It is theoretically possible, that is, that we invaded Iraq solely to secure reserves for Big Oil and services contracts for Halliburton and Bechtel. I don't believe this. At least, I believe the evidence isn't yet sufficient to convict. But it will be interesting to get to the moment – early in the next Administration, let's presume – when the Energy Task Force archives open and we can know for sure.

It's more likely, though, that Cheney simply applied the doctrine of resource control with which he grew up to today's world – without thinking about what the global economy means.

Today, there is only one major communist country in the world – the People's Republic of China. But twenty-five years after it began economic reforms, China is thoroughly integrated into the dollar world. Does China have a problem getting oil? Not at all. Nor will it, so long as Chinese goods sell on American markets and oil can be bought for dollars. So who benefits from our expenditure of blood and treasure on the oil fields? Answer: so long as it works, anyone with whom we do business. Including China, of course, even though not a single PLA soldier need ever set foot away from Chinese soil.

The problem is, it doesn't work. The effort to control the fields phys-ically is leading, very rapidly, to increasing oil prices, a permanent volatility of supply – and to an inflationary slowdown in economic activity both in the United States and abroad. The implications are simple. Any security system that permits oil to come to market in an orderly way, we can live with. Any security system that inhibits this, we can't. The West can, and does, buy oil from the Iranian 'moolahs'. We can, and did, buy oil from Saddam. We buy it from the Saudis, whose misuse of the revenues includes, of course, the financing of a global network of terror. Issues of security are raised by each and every one of these cases. None of the Middle East oil regimes is security-safe. But the security risks can't be dealt with by physical occupation of the oil fields.

Obviously, Cheney doesn't get this, at all.

(*Salon*, 5 October 2004)

Waiting to Vote

COLUMBUS, Ohio – The real scandal of this election became clear to me at 6.30 p.m. on election day as I drove a young African-American voter, a charming business student, seven months pregnant, to her polling place at Finland Elementary School in south Columbus. We arrived in a squalling rain to find voters lined up outside for about a hundred yards. Later the line moved indoors. We were told that the wait had averaged two hours for the entire day. By the time the doors closed at 7.30 p.m., it was considerably longer.

Why such a line? Yes, turnout was a factor. But the real problem was a grotesque shortage of voting machines. Finland Elementary serves three precincts: Ward 37, A, B and C. The election officer at the door told me that the smallest of these precincts has some 400 registered voters, the middle-sized one has more than 800 and the largest 'thousands'. Because of the length and complexity of the ballot, voters were being limited to five minutes to finish their ballot, and most were using all that time. Each precinct had two functioning voting machines. The largest precinct was supposed to have three machines. One was broken at the precinct's opening and later replaced with another machine that also did not function. It's not hard to do the math. Five minutes per voter means 12 voters per machine per hour. Ohio polls were open for 13 hours, for a maximum throughput of 156 voters per machine, or 312 voters per precinct. That's barely enough for a 75 percent turnout in the smallest precinct of the three. For the larger precincts, it was a joke – on voters.

This situation played out all over the city of Columbus and the state of Ohio on election day, with lines reported at 90 minutes to two hours from start to finish. One of my drivers spent two-and-a-half hours accompanying a single elderly voter to the polls. How high was the turnout really? I don't yet know the answer to that. But I do know that you cannot judge from the lines. You have to know the number of machines and the time it takes to vote.

The miracle was the mood of the voters. They arrived in all their all-American splendor – work clothes and sweat suits, ponchos and umbrellas, baby packs and walkers – with almost infinite patience and good humor. As I wrote this, waiting in the car at 8 p.m. a half-hour after the polls officially closed, perhaps 300 more were still waiting inside the school. Most of them likely stayed there until they could vote. My young friend also toughed it out.

Were the long lines the result of incompetence? Of insufficient funding for the new touch-screen machines? Or were they part of a strategy to discourage and suppress the vote? I report; you decide. But whatever the reason, the failure to provide enough machines for Americans to vote without having to wait for two hours or more is a scandal.

(*Salon*, 3 November 2004)

Abolish Election Day

1. Was this election stolen?

The Internet is alive with furious messages from my frustrated friends, fanning the flames of Florida 2000. Many have zeroed in on the discrepancy between the exit polls and the final results. How, they demand to know, could the leaks that so strongly favored John Kerry early in the evening have been so far wrong?

A comparison of the Florida vote with that of other Southern states gives little comfort to the case for fraud. As an exercise, I calculated an 'expected vote' for George Bush in Florida by taking his 2000 total and multiplying it by the growth in Florida's voting-age population. Bush exceeded this target by a large margin, 24 percent. But by the same standard he did equally well in Georgia and even better in Oklahoma and Tennessee – where there was no contest and no reason to miscount Bush's votes. In terms of improvement over 2000, Florida was Bush's fourth-best state. But his gains there weren't out of line with his gains over 2000 throughout the South.

Florida remained as close as it did because Kerry also improved on his 'expected vote' – by 12 percentage points. Gains by both candidates were possible because overall turnout in Florida increased 10 percentage points, from 47 to 56 percent of the voting-age population. That, too, was a big gain by national standards. But it was not as much as in seven other states – South Dakota, Minnesota, New Hampshire, Ohio, Nevada, Wisconsin and New Mexico – all of which were battleground states except South Dakota, where there was an important Senate fight.

How could the exit polls have failed to pick up Bush's surge? Here's a straightforward possibility: the exit-polling technique is to ask voters in selected precincts to record their votes on a ballot as they emerge from the polls. Not all voters are polled; rather, the pollster seeks a fixed fraction (say, every third voter) over a fixed time interval (say, 7 a.m. to noon for the morning poll).

If (as is usually the case) the polling places are operating below their capacity, then this technique will pick up two important aspects of the final total. First, it will accurately capture the relative vote for Bush and Kerry in each targeted precinct. Second, if turnout is higher than the past standard for that precinct, the poll will also show a higher count for that precinct, which gives the pollster a fighting chance to identify a turnout surge in one part of the state or another.

But suppose voting is much higher than expected. And suppose further that (for reasons to be discussed below), precincts are operating at their capacity – or, even worse, that their capacity has been reduced, relative to previous elections, because of a complicated ballot or short-age of machines. In that case, the exit pollster will not see the full increase in turnout during any fixed period of time. Instead, there will be a queue of voters, many of whom will actually vote only later, after the time window for the exit poll has closed. That element in the increased turnout will be missed. Since turnout did surge more in Florida's red than blue counties, this is a sufficient explanation for the failure of the exit polls there, unless something further and heinous comes to light. Don't count on it.

Let's turn to Ohio. Here Greg Palast – a journalist whose work cannot be disregarded – argues flatly that Kerry won the election in Ohio, and also in New Mexico, though the latter does not matter. Palast's logic does not rest on exotica – no hacking, no trap doors in the software are required – but rather on spoiled ballots. Palast points to the old Florida stand-by – hanging chads. Ohio this year used punch-card technology in 69 counties. The state lost 94,000 ballots to spoilage in 2000, according to a Harvard study. This year it lost 92,672. These ballots could be counted by hand. Alongside the chads, there are the provisional ballots issued to voters whose registration was questioned. Provisional ballots number around 155,000, according to recent reports, though earlier estimates were higher.

Bush won the counted vote in Ohio by 136,000 votes. If Kerry won 247,000 uncounted votes by 78 percent, then he won Ohio, the Electoral College and the Presidency. If only 155,000 provisional ballots are considered, of which 90 percent were valid, as was the case in 2000, then Kerry would need 99 percent of them – an impossibility. Practically speaking, Ohio will not recount automatically (including the 'spoiled' ballots) unless the margin closes to well under 20,000 – an event requiring Kerry to get 92 percent of the valid provisionals. And while a substantial Kerry majority among the provisional voters is likely, it's almost surely not as high as that. Since many red counties used punch cards, there is no clear reason to suppose Kerry enjoys an equally large lead as far as spoiled ballots are concerned.

In Ohio, where the increase in voter turnout favored both candidates almost equally, the exit polls were not so wrong. It was a very close race. At least one identified case of vote miscounting (in Gahanna, Ohio, favoring Bush by almost 4000 votes) has been acknowledged. Other serious allegations have been made. All in all, therefore, the demand that all Ohio's votes be counted before the electors are certified is a reasonable one. However, it remains true that the odds against overcoming Bush's present lead in votes cast are fairly decisive.

2. Was the election fair?

The vote in Ohio raised another issue, yet more serious for the future. Was the election conducted fairly? And, in particular, what effect did new machine technologies, used in many parts of the state, have on the vote? That forces us to consider the votes that were not cast.

Kerry did very well in Ohio. By the method described in the previous section, he exceeded his 'expected vote' – based on Al Gore's 2000 performance – by 19 full percentage points. This was better than Bush's gains in the state, which were 17 points above expected values, in a state where turnout rose by just under 10 full percentage points, from 53 to nearly 63 percent. Kerry's campaign had a terrific ground operation, which had canvassed his strong neighborhoods repeatedly and knew his voters. If Kerry lost the state, it was because Bush did just well enough so that Kerry could not quite overcome the deficit with which he'd started. Yet – as I wrote earlier – a scandal of this election became clear to me personally at 6.30 p.m. on election day, as I drove a first-time voter to her polling place in south Columbus. We arrived to find voters lined up outside, three and four across, for about a hundred yards, in the rain. Later the line moved indoors; we were told that the wait had averaged two hours for the entire day. By the time the doors closed at 7.30 p.m., it was considerably longer.

Why such a line? The turnout – on average in the state, 20 percent above the previous base – was a factor. But in Franklin County high turnout was entirely in line with rising registrations, and the Election Commission obviously knew about it. The real problem was a grotesque shortage of voting machines. At Finland Elementary, where three precincts voted, an election officer told me that the smallest had some 400 registered voters, the middle-sized one had more than 800, and the largest had 'thousands'. Voters were being limited to five minutes to finish their ballot, and because of its length and complexity most were using the full time.

Each precinct had two functioning voting machines. The largest precinct was supposed to have three machines. One was broken at the opening, and later replaced with another machine that also did not function. Five minutes per voter means 12 voters per machine per hour. Ohio polls were open for 13 hours, for a maximum throughput of 156 voters per machine, or 312 voters per precinct in this case. That's barely enough for a 75 percent turnout in the smallest precinct of the three. And the lines for all three precincts were jumbled together – so even if your machine was ready for you, you had to wait.

This situation played out all over the city of Columbus on election day, with lines reported at 90 minutes to two hours from start to finish. One of my drivers spent two-and-a-half hours accompanying a single elderly voter to the polls. Commentators marveled at the turnout. But you cannot judge from the lines. You have to know the number of machines and the time it takes to vote. In relation to registrations, turnout in Franklin County was only 2 percent higher in 2004 than in 2000 – by far the lowest proportionate gain of any major county in Ohio. While Kerry won Franklin County, he could have done much better. Vote suppression worked, in the face of the greatest get-out-the-vote drive I've ever seen. Raising the increase in turnout of registered voters to 10 percent (as happened in Cuyahoga County) would not have made the difference in the state.

Nevertheless: it is an injustice, an outrage and a scandal – a crime, really – that American citizens should have to wait for hours in the November rain in order to exercise the simple right to vote.

3. Vote-by-mail: the time has come

The remedy is voting by mail, the system now in place in the state of Oregon. In Oregon, there are no election day problems, because there is no election day. Instead, ballots are mailed to voters at their registered address, filled out and returned, with a signature verification. Participation rates are high – 63 percent of the voting age population this year, against a national average of 53 percent. Fraud is virtually nil. And as the ballots are paper (they are read by a scanning machine), there is a verifiable paper trail.

Incidentally, Kerry did very well in Oregon. He beat his 'expected vote' there by 17 percent, while Bush beat his by only 9 percent. Kerry's gain relative to Bush's in Oregon was his fifth-best overall and the best, for him, of any significant state. Thus Kerry sharply improved on Gore's narrow win in Oregon. It's likely that the fact that votes were cast early – closer to the debates and before the final advertising onslaughts – played an important role in this result. But this is not a partisan effect; the Democratic debate advantage is not an institutional matter. Had Bush won the debates, he likely would have sewed up the election immediately, under vote-by-mail.

Taking the Oregon system to the national level would have several dramatic effects. Voting would start weeks before the election day; thus the importance of an effective political organization to register voters and insure their participation would rise. Meanwhile, the role of advertising would decline. Late advertisements, which are often highly misleading, would be seen mainly by those who had already cast their votes. 'October surprises', such as the late appearance of Osama bin Laden in the 2004 election, would lose their importance, for the same reason.

On election day there would be no bottlenecks at the polls, because there would be no polls. All the money spent on election officials would be saved. So would much now spent on voting machines. Only enough would be required to count ballots, over a period of weeks, at a central location in each county. Election day challenges and get-out-the-vote drives would end. Private corporations and their occult vote-counting machinery would be driven out of the elections business, into which they should never have been allowed to enter. The atmosphere of low-grade thuggery and suspicion that now surrounds the act of voting in many places would disappear. So would the corrosive doubts about the integrity of the outcome.

But most of all – and most wonderfully – vote-by-mail would end the practice of exit polls and the reporting of partial counts. And with that would end the noxious night of watching the networks pontificate about an outcome on which they have privileged, though usually defective, information. Instead, each state would report its tally when, at the end of the evening, the count is completed. There would be a relatively brief window of great excitement. Then the election would be over. And the result would be known. For sure.

Vote-by-mail could be put in place by a simple act of Congress, setting appropriate standards, or by state legislatures acting one by one. Unlike Electoral College reform it is not a constitutional matter. It would place voting on the same basis as filing taxes or filling out the census – processes no one supposes to be perfect, but that are largely handled with minimal and acceptable error. Instituting the Oregon system should be the first priority for electoral reform in the years ahead. It is the only way, currently available, to assure both the right to vote and the right to a clean and accurate count.

(*The Nation* online at thenation.com, 29 November 2004)

Democracy Inaction

The election was stolen. That's not in doubt. Secretary of State Colin Powell admitted it. The National Democratic Institute and the International Republican Institute both admitted it. Senator Richard Lugar of Indiana – a Republican – was emphatic: there had been 'a concerted and forceful program of Election Day fraud and abuse', he 'had heard' of employers telling their workers how to vote; yet he had also seen the fire of the resisting young, 'not prepared to be intimidated'.

In Washington, former National Security Adviser Zbigniew Brzezinski demanded that the results be set aside and a new vote taken, under the eye – no less – of the United Nations. In the *New York Times*, Steven Lee Myers decried 'the use of government resources on behalf of loyal candidates and the state's control over the media' – practices, he said, that were akin to those in 'Putin's Russia'.

Personally, I don't know whether the *Ukrainian* election was really stolen. I don't trust Lugar, Powell or the National Democratic Institute. It's obvious that US foreign policy interests, rather than love of democracy for its own sake, are behind this outcry. Russia backed the other candidate in Ukraine. For Brzezinski, doing damage to Russia is a hobby.

But if the Ukraine standard were applied in Ohio – as it should be – then the late lamented US election certainly was stolen. In Ohio, the secretary of state in charge of the elections process was co-chairman of the Bush campaign in the state. He obstructed the vote count systematically – for instance, by demanding that provisional ballots without birth dates on their envelopes be thrown out, even though there is no requirement for that in state law. He also required that provisional ballots be cast in a voter's home precinct, ensuring that there would be no escape from long lines. Republicans fielded thousands of election challengers to Democratic precincts, mainly to try to intimidate black voters and to slow down the voting process. A recount, demanded and paid for by the Green and Libertarian parties, has been stalled in court, so that it won't possibly upset the certification of Ohio's electoral votes.

In Franklin County, Ohio, there was rampant abuse, with voting machines added in Republican precincts and taken away in Democratic ones, as documented by the *Columbus Dispatch*. The result was a crippling pile-up at the polls; many thousands did not vote because they simply could not afford to wait. I witnessed this with my own eyes. And Senator Lugar could have, too, for much less than the price of airfare to Kiev. According to an article by Bob Fitrakis and Harvey Wasserman:

> The man running the show in Franklin County was Board of Elections Director Matt Damschroder, former head of the county's Republican Party . . . Damschroder's official records also show that while desperate poll workers called his office throughout the day, at least 125 machines were held back at the opening of the polls and an additional 68 were never deployed. Thus while thousands of inner city voters stood in the rain, were told their cars would be towed, and were then forced to vote in five minutes or less, Damschroder sat on machines that could have significantly sped the process.[1]

These are the established facts. Eyewitness reports of other forms of abuse include malfunctioning voting machines in Youngstown, a mysterious lockdown of the vote count in Warren County and lesser incidents that run into the thousands. And then there are allegations of irregularities in the count – how solid these are, one does not know. Taken together, are these enough to change the outcome? No one can say. But the same is true in Kiev. And there, allegations by the defeated opposition are taken in good faith, and are quite enough to satisfy international observers and the government of the United States.

So where is the press? Why aren't there more stories on Ohio? Why is there no national pressure for a prompt statewide recount? Why no continuing outcry? Why no demand – as our friends are making with strong American support in Ukraine – that the election results in Ohio be set aside and a new vote held? Why has our election, with all its thuggery, been forgotten just three weeks after it occurred?

One reason, of course, is that the US government gives direction in these matters, here at home as well as around the world. And our press, like that in 'Putin's Russia' follows suit. Our political leaders, if one could call them that, stay silent and move on. They are terrified of being mocked and bullied by the press.

Another reason is that in Ohio, pissed-off voters are well behaved. They are working the hearings process, the recount process and the unhearing, unseeing courts. In Kiev, by contrast, hundreds of thousands of demonstrators are on the streets, staying there overnight in the bitter cold, bringing the government to a halt and the world to attention.

We'll get our democracy back, one of these days, when the Democratic Party has a mass base and is prepared to use it in the same way.

Note

1. At http://www.tompaine.com/articles/kerry_won_.php.

(*Salon*, 30 November 2004)

The Floodgates Have Opened

James K. Galbraith and Michael D. Intriligator

Hurricane Katrina and the death of New Orleans have changed everything, exposing the rot in government and the failures of the free-market worldview that has dominated our politics and economic policy for more than 30 years. Once again, the country must take stock of a terrible failure; once again we must change direction.

It is becoming clear that the human and economic damage from Katrina will far exceed that from September 11. Katrina has killed thousands[1] and displaced more than a million people. Immediately they need shelter, food, clothing, medical care, and places in school; these are being provided. But very quickly they will also need housing, jobs, and health insurance. Later on they will need help to get back home, if they choose to return, as many will, when New Orleans and the Gulf Coast are rebuilt.

The affected families should be given housing vouchers and placement assistance; cities like Houston, which is inundated with evacuees, should get immediate impact aid to provide housing units, classrooms, and, if required, jobs. All Gulf Coast evacuees should get immediate health coverage under Medicare. And let's help the evacuees form a national union, to communicate with one another, to represent their interests, and to keep alive the spirit of New Orleans and the Gulf Coast. In our democracy, the voices of the displaced must be heard.

To rebuild New Orleans and the Gulf Coast will require a vast and coordinated effort. Before the storm, scientists and planners called for $14 billion to rehabilitate the barrier islands and wetlands and to re-engineer the levees. Rebuilding the city itself will cost tens of billions more. And it should be done fairly soon in the interest of those just displaced. The new New Orleans should be a beacon of mixed neighborhoods, affordable housing, and decent transit for the poor and middle class. It should be free of slumlords and protected from excessive gentrification. Because the risks will not go away, the country needs a new disaster-management paradigm. This must include transparent plans, properly resourced, with provision for all Americans living in areas of risk.

The Federal Emergency Management Agency, or FEMA – which was functional under Bill Clinton and corrupted under George W. Bush – must be taken out of the Department of Homeland Security and given back over to competent leadership. But that should be only the beginning; it is very clear we are totally unprepared to cope with calamity on the scale just seen. For the Gulf Coast we may need a new authority altogether – a Gulf Coast Authority, modeled on the Tennessee Valley Authority (TVA) and based in the region – to manage the ecological risks and coordinate disaster planning.

Katrina's damage extends nationwide. Oil production, refining, and trade routes are disrupted; prices are soaring; confidence is damaged. The Port of New Orleans cannot be dispensed with, and so long as it is disrupted the national economy is in peril. The best support will come not from quick fixes but from immediate steps that meet long-term needs, strengthening our infrastructure in many parts of the country after decades of neglect and decay.

But some quick fixes are needed. On the physical side, opening and staffing the port will have to be done quickly at any cost. On the human side, the new bankruptcy bill should be suspended at once, before it takes effect on October 17. Gulf Coast evacuees who have lost everything should get immediate relief from their existing debts.

So then, where must the resources come from? It's obvious that immediate relief, long-term investment needs, and a slowing economy will all add to deficits and debt. So be it: meeting needs must take precedence over all other objectives right now. But even so, resources can be found to cover part of the cost.

First, the National Guard must come home from Iraq, and our adventure there phased out as soon as it safely can be. Congress should also kill the Missile Defense program, bunker-busting nuclear weapons, proposed permanent bases in Iraq, Afghanistan, and Central Asia, and other military systems that add nothing to our security. Bridges to nowhere in Alaska and other civilian pork should be cut immediately. Steel and concrete are needed, now, for more important things.

Next, Congress must declare a moratorium on all tax cuts. The estate tax should be restored at a fair level, not repealed, as the Senate leadership continues to propose, at a cost of $1.5 billion a week. The IRS and financial regulators should shut down offshore tax havens and bring those who have abused them to justice. New taxes as necessary should fall on those who can afford to pay: on capital gains, dividends, and those with high incomes. It was poor and middle-class citizens who, above all, suffered catastrophe last week. Prosperous Americans must now share the burden of helping them out.

Finally – as if the above were not enough – we will need to focus on getting rid of corruption in this country at every level: state, local and federal. Looting is indeed intolerable. But it's very clear that the worst looting we've seen has been the wholesale destruction of the capacity – and indeed the will – of the government to serve the people. The shocking misconduct of FEMA during the disaster, when timely and determined action could have saved many lives, needs a full and completely independent investigation. One vignette, disclosed by Senator Mary Landrieu on September 3, tells much: that in the midst of the disaster, Bush's minions faked the repair of the 17th Street canal levee in New Orleans for a presidential photo opportunity. The changes we need now go to the heart of this mentality. That will require not only the defeat of the present Administration, but a fundamental break with complacency, cynicism, and indifference in both parties.

Note

1. We learned later that early death estimates were high; the immediate death toll was in the order of one thousand.

(The American Prospect, September 2005)

About War

National Defense

A few observations on the events of September 11 and their aftermath.

First, the horror did not make the American people lose their minds. Reaction everywhere was calm, dedicated, and in New York City and at the Pentagon, heroic. Ugly incidents against Arab-Americans or Islamic religious sites were overshadowed by solidarity expressed on both sides. By and large, any fellow citizen had to be proud of our own.

The events distinguished quite sharply between officials. Mayor Giuliani behaved splendidly. Secretary Rumsfeld showed personal stature by staying on the scene during the immediate crisis. ABC News stood out for calm reporting – Peter Jennings and John Miller especially – free of the offensive banner slogans of the other networks, and avoiding pornographic repetition of the scenes from Tuesday morning. Senator Biden spoke with common sense about the limitations of force in reaction.

Not many others reached that standard. While sorrow swept the country, war fever swept the Beltway. Our political leaders personalized the attacks, promised what they cannot deliver, and demanded a deference to their judgment that they have not earned. On TV, Sam Donaldson and many others bayed for blood – the more the better and never mind whose. The call to war was, nevertheless, a calculated one, shifting the burden of response from the police, FBI, diplomats and foreign governments to our military forces.

Yet talk of war by week's end was already leading to hard questions. War against whom? With what means? At what cost? Afghanistan is a mountainous, land-locked country described pungently by one officer as 'not target-rich'. Bombs kill civilians, but they are unlikely to find bin Laden. Small groups of soldiers can be sent, but what would they do? How would they get out? A force to depose the Taliban would be a service to humanity, and to Afghanistan. But by informed accounts it would not affect bin Laden's network very much.

What did we learn about that network? That it is imbedded partly in the United States – in Florida, in Boston. That it used small groups armed with knives and limited flight training to turn civil aircraft into flying bombs: low cost for high effect. That it chose vulnerable targets, as the World Trade Center was known to be; there are probably not many places where equal numbers could be killed. And, even at the Trade Center, many did escape. The Pentagon, on the other hand, proved quite robust under attack.

The attacks themselves were near things. They depended on passive responses by the pilots and passengers, and they failed on United 93 once those on board learned what had happened in New York. In any event, simple measures (marshals, stronger doors, better airport security teams) would deter or defeat the identical effort in future. Threats of other kinds will emerge, but the methods of September 11 revealed something about the limits to, as well as the potential for, terror on US soil – so far. Complacency is not justified; neither is panic.

The American people did not panic; sadly the financial markets were another story. The authorities ran a thoughtless risk in reopening the New York Stock Exchange after six days, with uncertain infrastructure, exhausted operatives and nerves severely on edge. Their reward was a sharp sell-off on the first day. The rush to reopen added a distraction we didn't need, raising anxieties, and for no larger economic or social purpose.

A prolonged run on US markets could, in turn, cause problems for recovery efforts down the road. These will require very large amounts of public money – goodbye lockbox, goodbye surplus. Will the US – until Tuesday the world's ultimate good credit – still be seen that way if stock prices and the dollar continue to fall? Can our trade deficit and our appetite for oil coexist with the pressures of new deficits to finance a war, the recovery effort, and – very soon – a fight against recession?

If not, we may soon face deep realities about our dependence on oil, and so about our very presence in the Arab world, against which these attacks were directed. That presence is not a fact of nature. It is, rather, the result of fifty years of commercial, industrial and strategic decisions. To change now would be a large task – to rebuild our cities, our transport, and our patterns of housing and our industrial base, as well as to reduce (rather than expand) our military exposure in the wider world. Few have yet focused on such essentially defensive measures. But they may be required, if the war proves long and difficult (as it probably will) or if, as one can only fear, it spreads through the Persian Gulf.

And so, fellow citizens, we'd better start thinking about all that, pretty soon – even as we mourn and honor our dead.

(*The Texas Observer*, September 2001)

The Future Oil War

Let me state in passing my view that UT's President Faulkner should not have attacked my colleague Bob Jensen in the early days following September 11, for Jensen's hot objections to the use of US military force in Afghanistan (and elsewhere). True, Faulkner's words didn't bother Jensen much, and no concrete steps were taken against him. But, given Faulkner's position, he may have sent a signal to others on campus, less secure in their jobs than Bob is, and this is something that a university president should always avoid.

That said, as events have unfolded, it does not appear that Jensen's position has been borne out. As I write, in half the country of Afghanistan, the war is nearly over. The Taliban has fled Mazar-e-Sharif, Taliqan, Herat, and is on the verge of quitting Kabul. As the militia left Mazar, the residents picked up Kalashnikovs to hurry them along, a sign of civic sentiment. Schools for girls can now reopen.

The UN Food Program, having warned of critical shortages, now states that supply lines can be reopened in the North, giving hope that famine will be averted. Without the war, the famine risk there was already serious, and the resources for dealing with that now will be greater than they would have been. While civilians have been killed, one cannot fairly argue that the US targeted this campaign against civilians – as it did do, unmistakably, in Iraq and in Serbia. Most of the recent attacks were on troop lines. Afghanistan is not Vietnam, neither in topography, in politics nor military tactics.

So, for the moment the judgment of the soldiers looks pretty good. The main risks now lie a little further on. We will have to control our allies. The Northern Alliance in particular has a bad track record, which is how the Taliban got to power in the first place. Still, so did the Bosnian Serbs, yet they haven't much messed with American troops, or with civilians, since we got there. If I were a Pat Buchanan isolationist, intent on keeping US soldiers away from liberal-do-good nation-building programs, I'd be more worried than I am right at the moment.

And one has to remember that the Russians got into so much trouble in Afghanistan partly because of us. This war is, to some extent, to clean up the mess left by the CIA. If it takes the Air Force and the Rangers to do that – well, sometimes you have to. In that regard, the shocking report on Radio France International on October 31 that a CIA operative had direct contact with bin Laden in July of this year at the American Hospital in Dubai deserves vigorous investigation. Which, of course, it will not get.

So, let us suppose that the Afghan war continues to go well and let us hope that the impending occupation is comparatively benign. The question remains: what next? Even full victory in Afghanistan can not eliminate Al Qaeda, let alone the unfriendly Mr Saddam Hussein in Iraq. Moreover we can expect a blow-up in Saudi Arabia sooner or later, to add to the troubles of the oil patch.

Hubbert's Peak, the new book by Kenneth Deffeyes (Princeton, 2001), tells us what is at stake in the Middle East: a petrochemical reserve of limitless value in an age when world production will start declining quite soon. The social philosopher Richard Cheney has told us that we are at the beginning of an age of unending war. Cheney isn't very social, and he doesn't know philosophy. But he surely understands the geophysics and the politics of oil.

So, look down the road: nightmare scenarios come readily to mind. The Middle East has most of the world's oil, and as production falls the Middle East's share of the remaining reserves will rise. At home, if we pay a rising *dollar* price, it could mean an essentially endless depression. Think the 1970s, without Jimmy Carter for leadership and comfort.

But there is another possibility. We could control the dollar price, so that the oil shortfall remains largely invisible to the American consumer. One has to believe that this idea has occurred to the oil men in charge. The problem then is that conditions elsewhere would then be much worse. For this strategy implies pricing developing countries out of the market by driving their currencies down. This can be done by driving a hard bargain on their debts. Eventually, irrigation pumps will run dry, and the Green Revolution would start running backwards. From the standpoint of the developing world, the game is zero-sum; our success in a war for control is their descent into famine.

And either way, on top of the reserve, the financial wealth of Saddam and the Saudis would grow, alongside the attractiveness of those regimes as targets for war and revolution – or for outright military occupation by the United States. Cheney's forecast, under these circumstances, is realistic. And his policy, which appears to be to fight for and maintain control of oil, fits exactly to the interests of the companies and also, sad to say, the short-term economic interest of the American middle class.

Unfortunately, however, it is also a formula for abandoning those countries on whose cooperation our security now depends. The result: we could face, quite soon, an endless war for a diminishing resource, in which every victory for the American motorist starves a Bengali, an Indonesian, or an Afghan. This outcome is unlikely to bring peace – think Israel and the Arabs on a global scale.

And what is the alternative? There is one, but it would involve finding our way away from over-reliance on oil, back to a mixed economy built around human needs, and back toward a system of regulated development under multilateral control at sustainable interest rates, wiping the slate of unpayable debts built up over thirty years, and managing the oil reserve for the benefit of the whole world.

This could happen; it is almost unfortunate that the easy victories in Afghanistan make it less likely. Don't expect serious progress until the scope of the war still ahead becomes more clear. And by then, of course, for many people it will be too late.

(*The Texas Observer*, 23 November 2001)

The Cheney Doctrine

Mr Cheney's speech of August 26th provides us with the fullest statement we are likely to get in justification of an attack on Iraq. Whether it represents the final word in Bush Administration policy is anyone's guess; press reports afterward suggested that the speech was neither fully cleared with the White House nor fact-checked with the CIA. Still, it seems unlikely that Mr Bush will be able to make a stronger case. Let us, therefore, work with what we've got, in the short time that apparently remains.

To begin with, we may concede what is indisputable. Saddam Hussein is a dictator and an enemy. He has used chemical and perhaps also bio-weapons on his own population, in addition to murdering tens of thousands in conventional ways. His demise would be welcomed by most Iraqis. Much of his army would not fight, and the part that would cannot be thought a major military opponent. Further, while no one can be sure, the costs to civilians of a swift invasion might prove tolerably low. In Afghanistan, even though far too many innocents were killed, American military forces nevertheless did a better job with fewer such casualties than many feared. They can be expected to conduct an Iraqi war with as much respect for the risks to civilians as intelligence, planning and the technologies allow.

On grounds of human rights, therefore, active US military support for an Iraqi revolt might be justified. This might particularly be the case if the result in prospect were enduring security for the northern Kurds of Iraq and self-determination for the southern Shi'a, who together make up a large majority of Iraq's population. The Shi'a in particular would be major beneficiaries of a regime change, since unlike the Kurds they do not presently control their own territories and do not live in safety from Saddam's forces.

But human rights, democracy and self-determination are not the grounds advanced by Mr Cheney for an attack on Saddam. The break-up of Iraq into self-governing cantonments is particularly not among Cheney's objectives. Greater independence for the Kurds would gravely offend our ally Turkey, while self-determination for the Shi'a would give satisfaction to Iran, a charter member of the 'axis of evil'. Nor would most Americans – either on the left or the right – accept these purposes as sufficient reason to go to war.

And so, Mr Cheney seeks to justify a military invasion of Iraq instead *on grounds of the national security of the United States*. His speech emphasizes the threat posed by Saddam Hussein to ourselves. These stem from his pursuit of chemical, biological and nuclear weapons, his concealment of that pursuit, his persistent plotting to foil and frustrate UN inspectors, and his appalling past record of regional aggression, against Iran and then against Kuwait. Cheney wraps these factors into a frightening bundle of conclusions:

> Should all [Saddam's] ambitions be realized, the implications would be enormous for the Middle East, for the United States, and for the peace of the world. The whole range of weapons of mass destruction then would rest in the hands of a dictator who has already shown his willingness to use such weapons, and has done so, both in his war with Iran and against his own people. Armed with an arsenal of these weapons of terror, and seated atop ten percent of the world's oil reserves, Saddam Hussein could then be expected to seek domination of the entire Middle East, take control of a great portion of the world's energy supplies, directly threaten America's friends throughout the region, and subject the United States or any other nation to nuclear blackmail.

From this it is a short step to the doctrine of pre-emptive self-defense. Saddam Hussein is an ambitious, aggressive, dangerous man, with access to vast wealth and technical capacities. Mr Cheney claims that 'without doubt' he currently possesses 'weapons of mass destruction'. There is therefore a threat that he will some day soon choke off our access, and that of our friends and allies, to the oil on which we rely, and then defend his position with 'nuclear blackmail'. Therefore, Mr Cheney concludes, *we must act*, lest by waiting we find that we are helpless against the man and the weapons he may soon control.

It is, on the surface, an impressive argument. We face a threat. Why wait? Time, as the Administration likes to say, is not on our side. It all seems on first reading entirely persuasive. And yet it is not. There are two holes in the argument. One of them concerns the facts. The other the underlying question of principle.

In the first place, the supposed facts which Mr Cheney advances may not be true. Mr Cheney is not a reliable source. On the contrary, he is a notorious liar, well known for fitting factual claims to predetermined conclusions. (A review of Mr Cheney's advocacy of the missile defense system provides ample proof of this point.) Mr Cheney presents no actual evidence in defense of his claims. And we are advised that in the preparation of his speech, Mr Cheney did not seek a review of his facts from intelligence specialists in our own government.

Further, some matters presented as fact by Mr Cheney are simply not within his power to know. We do not know, because we cannot know, what Saddam's regional ambitions are, at this point in his career. We do know that asserting those ambitions with conventional military forces would be very difficult for Saddam today. Today he controls barely two-thirds of his own country, and half of that only in daylight hours. The Iraqi military is smaller and considerably weaker than it was twelve years ago. Iraqi airplanes cannot fly over much of their own territory, owing to the no-fly zones. The Iraqi army did poorly in recent skirmishes against the Kurds. It could not today take a war to Iran, or even once again overrun Kuwait, given our presence and instant opposition. It certainly could not take the oil fields of Saudi Arabia, Therefore the claim that Iraq might come to dominate the 'entire Middle East', and then defend its conquests with weapons of mass destruction, is absurd.

Other alleged facts are less impressive than Mr Cheney claims. Take the statement that Saddam 'now has weapons of mass destruction'. What does this mean? No one is claiming that Saddam possesses the atomic bomb; the testimony of defectors and the evidence from UNSCOM concur that his nuclear program did not succeed in acquiring the essential ingredient, namely bomb-grade uranium or plutonium. Chemical and biological weapons he may still have. But, however frightening, they do not pose a similar threat. Suppose Saddam does possess, in hidden warehouses, vials of anthrax, Sarin, VX and mustard gas? What would he do with them? How militarily effective have these weapons ever proved to be? What do we have to fear from them, especially in small quantities? Something, to be sure. But probably not so much, for instance, as from airliners bearing down on tall buildings. And there is no evidence that Iraq was involved in that.

But the underlying principle does not depend on whether Mr Cheney's combination of psychological inference, history and current information is correct. Mr Cheney's argument is not that the reality of the Saddam threat has been proved. It is, rather, than we are entitled to act on presumption and inference. Mr Cheney holds that our responsibility is to assume the worst, and to act today, in order to prevent the worst, on the off-chance that the assumption is correct.

This is the meaning of the declaration, at the outset of the August 26th speech as well as at West Point and elsewhere by Mr Bush, that the 'old doctrines of security do not apply'. Mr Cheney clarifies:

> In the days of the Cold War, we were able to manage the threat with strategies of deterrence and containment. But it's a lot tougher to deter enemies who have no country to defend. And containment is not possible when dictators obtain weapons of mass destruction, and are prepared to share them with terrorists who intend to inflict catastrophic casualties on the United States.

Here is the core premise of the Bush doctrine – a mantra repeated numerous times in speeches by Bush as well as Cheney. It is a point over which most commentators have passed in silence, in order to debate such secondary issues as whether UNSCOM really did, or really did not, neutralize Saddam's mass destructive threat, or whether Saddam really is, or really isn't, in any way connected to Al Qaeda. And what is most striking about this premise is its complete illogic and falsehood.

First, whatever the merit of Mr Cheney's assertion that deterrence is impotent where enemies 'have no country to defend', that statement does not apply to Saddam Hussein. Saddam does have a country. He *knows* that the use of chemical, biological or radiological weapons against ourselves, Israel, Kuwait or any allied country would bring on a rain of retaliatory ruin, from which he could not personally hope to escape. For this reason, he did not put chemical agents in the Scuds fired at Israel during the Gulf War. Deterrence worked perfectly at that moment. There is no reason to suppose it to be less effective today.

The claim that 'containment is not possible when dictators obtain weapons of mass destruction' is equally false on its face. What about the Soviet Union? That country, governed by dictators, had many such weapons. And yet it *was* contained, with great success, for four decades. The Soviet Union collapsed in the end without inflicting so much as a single external casualty from any one of these weapons. Nor did the Soviets ever contemplate sharing agents of mass destruction with terrorists, despite manifold Western fantasies (and James Bond movies) to that effect.

Yet there is a deeper reality behind the Bush-Cheney rejection of deterrence and containment, in favor of the doctrine of 'pre-emptive self-defense'. Their position is not a new one. It is very far from being a new idea, crafted by strategists thinking afresh about the world after the Cold War. It is, instead, a direct return to a fantasy of world domination, powered by the atomic monopoly, that took hold in American military minds in the immediate aftermath of World War II, and which threatened the security and survival of the world for twenty years after that.

The actual US nuclear war-fighting strategy – so far as the military understood it in the early 1960s – was that of a *pre-emptive and unprovoked* nuclear first-strike on the Soviet Union, using intercontinental ballistic missiles to destroy Soviet retaliatory capacity on the ground. Plans to this effect were presented to JFK in July, 1961, with a hypothetical strike date at the end of 1963. The plans had been drawn as they were, not because of a fear that deterrence and containment would not work. Rather, it was because the Soviets *lacked the capacity to strike at the United States*. And so, apart from the pressure on Berlin, which was resolved in 1961, and the brief crisis over missiles in Cuba, the Soviets posed no threat we needed to deter. The goal of our Single Integrated Operating Plan was to destroy them, on a suitable pretext, *before* they acquired the capability to strike at us.

'Deterrence' and 'containment' came into play only *after 1967*, when the Soviets finally deployed a viable strategic missile force. From that point forward, the strategies worked. *But it was then the United States, and not the Soviets, which came to be deterred and contained.*

Pre-emptive self-defense is nothing else than the most dangerous subterranean tendency of the Cold War bombardiers, Curtis LeMay and Thomas Power. It is the doctrine rightly ridiculed in *Dr Strangelove*, now resurrected as though it were a post-Cold War breakthrough. And this has happened only because Iraq, like the Soviets before 1967, is in no position to deter or contain the United States, and has no allies willing to do so on its behalf.

Before deterrence arrived, the high civilian leadership of the United States – especially Kennedy and Johnson, struggled for years to keep our nuclear forces under control. It was not easy. Afterwards Robert McNamara in particular didn't talk, while very few others knew. The true nature of Cold War deterrence thus remained a mystery to most

Americans, apart from glimpses in movies, such as *Thirteen Days* and this year's *K-19*. We prefer even now to think of our Minuteman missiles – if we think of them at all – as a defensive force, benign in intent, retaliatory in design, and arrayed against a comparable, yet more dangerous Soviet threat. Nothing of the sort was true.

These facts darken our historical reputation. But they cast no cloud over the traditional security doctrines. After 1967, mutual deterrence and containment did keep the Cold Peace. And this illustrates a general point about doctrine. A valid strategic doctrine must apply with equal power to the good, the bad, and the ugly. It must be reciprocal. It must preserve the peace in all directions. It must not be asymmetric – a valid doctrine for one nation-state, and not a valid doctrine for any other.

Pre-emptive self-defense fails this test. Mr Cheney claims for the United States the right to strike first, based on our inferences about intentions and capabilities of the foe. (Iraq is today's target. But what about China, a few years from now, after Taiwan – with undercover encouragement from the American far right – moves for independence in a few years? Will we assert a right to strike pre-emptively in Taiwan's defense?) Cheney conveys clear information as to our aggressive intentions. US capabilities are not in doubt. Nor is our possession of weapons of mass destruction. We also know that despite the intentions of the American military, and whatever weapons they use, an attack on Iraq will cost a minimum of thousands of innocent lives, and will inflict heavy damage on the civilian infrastructure of that country.

So does Mr Cheney concede that Iraq also has a right of pre-emptive self-defense? Does he concede the legitimacy of, say, a strike on American command-and-control centers at the Pentagon and the White House, should Saddam dream up some way to achieve this? And if not, on what basis could he formulate a complaint? From Saddam's point of view, the evidence of our intent, capability and imminent threat are clear. The only drawback is the practical one. Iraq, being far the weaker power, cannot assure that any surprise attack would achieve its purpose, namely that of crippling the American military threat to his regime.

It is interesting that this is just exactly the problem that the Japanese faced at Pearl Harbor. Admiral Yamamoto well knew that his surprise attack would only lead to disaster. Roosevelt knew this as well. But even knowing that Prime Minister Tojo (who either did not know, or did not care) would soon seek to strike a blow against us somewhere, Roosevelt did not seek to get in the first lick. He waited for the blow to fall. And in this way, the stigma of the 'date which will live in infamy' fell on them. And not on us.

Mr Cheney goes so far, in his speech, as to invoke the memory of December 7, 1941. He seems unaware of having stepped out of Roosevelt's shoes, and into Tojo's kimono. But history will not forgive him if he follows through. Ironically, since the balance of forces in truth is overwhelmingly on the American side, the end result in Iraq may be favorable, as it was in Afghanistan. But there will be a larger damage to American national interests, and to the safety and security of the world. And so history will not forgive us, either, if we let Mr Cheney and Mr Bush lead us to war on such terms.

(*The Texas Observer*, 11 October 2002)

The Unbearable Costs of Empire

Talk in Washington these days is of Rome. But George W. Bush is no Caesar, and France under Napoleon may be the better precedent. Like Bush, Napoleon came to power in a coup. Like Bush, he fought off a foreign threat, then took advantage to convert the Republic to Empire. Like Bush, he built an immense army. Like Bush, he could not resist the temptation to use it. But unlike Caesar's, Napoleon's imperial pretensions did not last.

Analogy is cheap, but the point remains. Empire is not necessarily destined to endure. And especially not in the undisturbed, vapid decadence to which our emperors so evidently aspire. True, in semi-modern times the British Empire lasted for a century or perhaps two, depending on how and what one counts. The Soviet Union held up for seven decades. But Napoleon was finished in just fifteen years.

There is a reason for this. To maintain an empire *against opposition* requires war – steady, unrelenting, unending war. And war is ruinous – from a legal, moral and also from an economic point of view. It can ruin the losers, such as Napoleonic France or Imperial Germany in 1918. And it can also ruin the victors, as it did the British and the Soviets in the twentieth century. And on the other hand, Germany and Japan recovered so well from World War II, in part because they were spared reparations and did *not* have to waste national treasure on defense in the aftermath of defeat.

The United States today is rich and prosperous. But this does not mean that we have the financial and material capacity to wage continuing war around the world. Even without war, Bush is already pushing the military budget up toward $450 billion per year. That's a bit over 4 percent of current GDP. A little combat – on say the Iraqi scale – could raise this figure by another $100 to $200 billion. A large war, such as might break out in a general uprising through the Middle East or South Asia, with the control of nuclear arsenals at stake, would cost much more, and could continue for a long time.

One is tempted to analyze these sums, and particularly the immediate costs of war in Iraq, in terms of budget deficits and interest rates – in terms, that is, of the conventional arithmetic of fiscal irresponsibility. But this would be a mistake. Fiscal irresponsibility *is* an important issue when one considers the Bush tax cut of 2001. If allowed to survive, that long-term program of relief for the rich will by itself ruin the federal fisc into the indefinite future. But the problem of toppling Saddam Hussein next year is not that the US will have difficulty selling bonds to pay for it. On the contrary, with our domestic economy in the dumps, with private business uninterested in investment, government bonds will sell easily. And even if they did not, the Federal Reserve itself could buy them. So too could the successor government in Iraq, which will have the oil with which to purchase, after the fact, its own accession to power. Either way, interest rates *need not* rise, and Bush's Iraq war will be timed to help, not hurt, the short-term performance of American growth and employment.

Nor is Bush's strategy necessarily irrational so far as it affects oil – in the short run. With a new Iraqi government, the US will gain an ally, prepared to help keep the oil price within the band that both US consumers and the remaining US producers can tolerate – low enough so as not fatally to drain purchasing power from the former, high enough so as not immediately to ruin the latter. Given the Bush-Cheney commitment to unlimited oil consumption, this will prove useful – in putting off a day of reckoning. For, if and as total world oil production declines – as credible scientific evidence suggests may start happening quite soon – the Middle East's share of the remaining reserves will rise. Normally, so too would the potential for cartel control and price manipulation. A robust US military presence in the oil fields, directly or by proxy, will naturally make this less of a danger.

In the short run, in other words, the Iraqi war could prove both stimulative and stabilizing. Unless the campaign goes badly or the neighborhood blows up, it is unlikely, in and of itself, to produce an immediate economic disaster. And so, the political opportunists – we may safely suppose they exist – who favor such a war *because* it might help rescue George W. Bush in 2004 may not be entirely wrong in their calculations.

But it would be wrong to conclude that all is therefore quiet on the war-economy front. The disaster will, instead, play out in at least two different ways over time.

The immediate problem of the Bush-Cheney war policy lies in the neglect and indifference, which it fosters, of all our other economic problems.

First, private business investment in the United States has now fallen virtually to the capital replacement level. There is no early prospect of revival, because the recession in *consumer spending* still lies ahead. Until that storm comes and passes, businesses will hold off on net new investment. As a result there will be little further application of new technologies to economic life. Instead, new technologists will be pulled back into the military sector, from whence they emerged thirty years ago, and the advanced private sector on which we have, until recently, based our hopes will wither.

Second, the recession in consumer spending cannot be put off forever. American households are still being crushed by debt. After September 11, their spending was held aloft by falling oil prices, falling interest rates, the tax rebate, rising government spending, and the auto companies' willingness to unload their inventories at a loss. For the moment, only the last factor remains, alongside a continuing bubble in the price of housing, supporting a continued flow of equity loans. The auto companies may give up their effort soon enough (right after the November election?) After that, the second loop of the 'W' recession will soon be on us in force.

Third, state and local government budgets continue to implode. Reasonable estimates now show $50 billion in deficits at the state level, and the losses are surely almost as large at the local level. As rainy-day funds are depleted, these will translate into service cuts, and sometimes into tax increases. Either way, household budgets will take the full hit. The war hysteria in Washington (alongside political cynicism, willful ignorance of the economics, defeatism and inertia) has so far blocked an effective campaign for revenue sharing, the one way in which the federal government might prevent this calamity this year.

Fourth, we have the day-to-day decline of our financial markets, which have already lost some $8.4 trillion in nominal shareholder value since the peak in 2000. To some extent, these losses are due to the corruption of certain major corporations, including several (not least, Halliburton) closely tied to the military-petroleum complex. Failure to attend to these issues is necessarily endemic in an Administration built on corporate fraud and committed to war for oil.

These problems cannot be cured so long as war remains our dominant political theme. But, serious though they are, they pale against the larger problem of the international trade and financial order under conditions of permanent war.

It is a straightforward fact that, if global oil production starts to decline but our consumption does not, that will require that *everyone else* cut their purchase and use of oil. But how can oil prices be held stable for Americans and yet made to rise for everyone else? Only by a policy of continuing *depreciation* in everyone else's currency. Such a policy of dollar hegemony amid worldwide financial instability, of debt deflation throughout the developing world, will make our trading partners' exports cheap, their imports dear, and keep their real wages low. It will be a policy, in short, of beggar-all-of-our-neighbors, while we live alone, in increasing idleness, inside the dollar bubble.

This is the policy which Bush and Cheney are actually imposing on the rest of the world. But they cannot make it last. It will make lives miserable elsewhere, generating ever more resistance, more terrorism, and ever more military engagement. Global depression makes our exports unprofitable, further undercutting activity at home. Meanwhile, we will not experience even gradual exposure to the changing energy balance, so that we will never make the investments required to adjust, even eventually, to a world of scarce and expensive oil. In the end, therefore, that world will arrive much more abruptly than it otherwise would, shaking the fragile edifice of our oil economy to the ground. And we will some day face a double explosion: of anger against our arrogance, and of actual shortage and collapsing living standards, when the confidence of investors in the dollar finally gives way.

Compared with this future, a new commitment to *collective* security, to a new world financial structure, to a rational energy and transportation policy, and to spending to meet our actual domestic needs would be a bargain. At the end of the Constitutional Convention Benjamin Franklin was asked what type of government the country would have. He famously replied, 'A republic, if you can keep it'. This remains very much the issue today. The author of *Poor Richard's Almanack* understood the economics very well.

(*The American Prospect*, 18 November 2002)

The Paramilitary Mind

In 1976 at the height of the Irish troubles I called on Conor Cruise O'Brien, then serving as Minister of Posts in the Irish Republic; his offices were in the Dublin Post Office of 1916 fame. I was on my way to Belfast, for no very good reason. In our brief meeting, O'Brien reflected bleakly on the fragility of peace efforts. It was so easy, he said, to bomb the negotiating table.

Now let us understand that people with the mentality of paramilitaries are, today, actually running the government of these United States. They have perfected the dual identity that once characterized the Ulster Unionists and the Protestant gangs, or Sinn Fein and the IRA. In public, they present themselves as world political leaders, as participants in the democratic forums of our own country and in the deliberative bodies of the world. And yet meanwhile, below the table, *the same people* direct an apparatus of violence in single-minded pursuit of their goals.

Thus on Iraq and at the United Nations our leaders speak of weapons of mass destruction. But it is plain that no amount of Iraqi disarmament could ever satisfy Mr Bush. He is bent on war and on the destruction of the Iraqi regime. War may begin at any time. Let us hope that the professional soldiers assigned to the task complete it as they undoubtedly wish – quickly, with as few military casualties, civilian deaths and as little physical destruction as possible. They will do their best, we may be fairly sure, in a situation they did not choose.

For the rest of us, the larger problem comes later. We will have to come to grips with an empire we do not want, with commitments we may not be able to escape. Will we soon depart from an Iraq that, under real democracy, would likely become an ally of Iran? Once our oil companies are in place? Given the implications for Israel? You tell me.

The exercise of preventive war, once undertaken, has momentous implications. We now know that North Korea has several routes to the atomic bomb: plutonium that may be reprocessed; Uranium-235 that may be separated with high-speed centrifuges acquired from Pakistan. They will take our willingness to fight one preventive war as willingness to fight another. The inevitable response? Production and dispersion of nuclear bombs.

The logic is implacable. North Korea, following America's lead on so many other matters, has withdrawn from the nuclear Non-Proliferation Treaty. The Korean bomb will probably exist in quantity, beginning within a matter of weeks. Once it does, nothing stops them from selling it.

And what, do you suppose, the Iranians are thinking? Wouldn't a few of those bombs be handy in defense of the Islamic Republic? North Korea needs the money. Iran has the money. Go figure. Imagine a quasi-permanent US occupation force in Iraq, under our present political leaders, next to a nuclear Iran.

Neither Iran, North Korea, nor even Iraq is an irrational state, bent on inflicting gratuitous and suicidal harm to the cities and civilians of the United States. In this respect they do not resemble the hijack squads of September 11. But we've already sent a clear message to the others: Saddam's problem was that he did not get the bomb soon enough. The best prospect for safety lies in a deterrent of one's own.

And yet, there is a problem with this reasoning. It presupposes a rational caution on the part of American leadership. It presupposes a leadership that will not respond with an even higher level of violence.

We now know – but far too few Americans really understand – that there was a long stretch of US history when only threads of sanity in the high civilian leadership – Presidents Kennedy and Johnson, and their advisers including Robert McNamara and my late friend, Walt Rostow – protected us from launching pre-emptive nuclear war against a nuclear-armed Soviet Union. Does that sanity still exist today? The example we're setting in Iraq will not be reassuring, either to North Korea or Iran.

In January of this year, I had the privilege of listening to McNamara describe, in hair-curling detail, what he had learned only a few months before about the disposition of Soviet tactical atomic weapons on Cuba in October, 1962. There were scores of them. Had we invaded Cuba then – as we were prepared to do and but for a lucky caution would have done – the holocaust would have started not with missiles but with torpedoes, fired from Soviet patrol boats at the invading fleet. Back in Washington at that time, nobody knew.

The lesson: in the nuclear age, you have to live with your enemies. You cannot safely destroy them. We are alive today in part because, forty years ago, our leaders understood this. But today, it appears they no longer do. They are taking us not just to war, but in all likelihood to a sequence of wars and war threats. Each will be one step closer to the atomic edge. The paramilitaries have bombed the negotiating table. It will take a long time to rebuild it, if we ever get the chance.

(*The Texas Observer*, 14 March 2003)

What Economic Price This War?

Recently as we debated the war now underway in Iraq, seven Nobel laureates joined 150 other US economists (including myself) to call for careful consideration of the costs of war in Iraq. When economists talk about costs, what do we mean? First, we mean budget costs – for gasoline, equipment, and explosives – that begin at about $100 billion. This figure is based on an assumption that the war goes well. If the assumption is wrong, the numbers will go up fast. The history of warfare – from Europe in 1914 to Vietnam in the 1960s – is littered with gross underestimates of budget costs.

We also mean the material costs, which are sometimes overstated in war – bombs may fall on empty fields or on rubble and damage can look worse than it is. In Iraq, though, the civilian population is already stressed. Even modest material damage – to the water, to the electric grids and the health system – could bring on humanitarian disaster. There are risks of sabotage, not least to the oil fields. And there will be some damage, inevitably, to the archeological heritage of Iraq and especially Baghdad.

The human costs are beyond accounting. No matter the number of casualities, every dead soldier, on either side, every dead civilian, is a human being who could have lived a productive and perhaps happy life. Every injured person will carry a burden of pain. We need not demean the grief ahead by trying to give it money value.

The uncertainty costs are more prosaic but just as hard to calculate. How much business investment, how much production, how much trade have we already lost – not only in the United States but in the world economy – because of the fear and uncertainty surrounding this war? What effect will war have on global economic decision-making, consumer and market confidence, global energy prices? How much more lies ahead?

The reconstruction costs are imponderable. One estimate for the cost of rebuilding Iraq runs to $2 trillion. But will the US actually do the job? What if it takes two years and 100,000 troops? Five years and 200,000 troops? What if the oil fields are shut down in the meantime?

The follow-on costs arise from the military situation we may face after the war ends. Will peace and democracy break out in Iraq? Will the war lead to peace, democracy, and demilitarization across the Middle East, as some believe? Or will there be rebellions, revenge killings, and proxy wars across Iraq, Syria, Saudi Arabia, and even Egypt? Not to mention in Israel and Palestine.

The diplomatic costs lie in the damage already done, and more may lie ahead – to relationships with Europe, Russia and other countries. One may count also the cost of disillusion, of much of the world's population, with the American ideal.

The opportunity costs are those that arise every time we make a decision to do one thing rather than another. By choosing to go to war, we are choosing to do less to solve our problems at home. We face a crisis in every state and local budget in this country – in every school, every welfare program, and every part of public health care. We face a crisis of trust in our corporations, and a crisis of confidence in the profitability of future business investment. American households are facing in slow motion a crisis of household debts. Little will be done about any of this, so long as we are preoccupied with war.

Finally, the apocalyptic costs should be considered. There is the risk, already unfolding, that North Korea will produce atomic bombs. There is also the risk that Iran will buy a few of them or make some of its own. There is the risk that we will shortly face one, two, or perhaps more nuclear powers who regard us – and not entirely without reason – as a mortal threat to their existence. There is the risk that we may make a catastrophic mistake in our response.

Once the real costs have been considered, the economic conclusion is not controversial. It is that collective security – the kind provided by strong alliances, the rule of law, and the United Nations Security Council – is the only real security. It is certainly the only kind that we, or any other country, can afford. Perhaps war is sometimes necessary. But it is never really cheap enough.

(*Boston Globe*, 24 March 2003)

Still Wrong: Why Liberals Should Keep Opposing the War

In a recent column, TAP online Editor Richard Just and tompaine.com Executive Editor Nick Penniman prescribed 'the only moral and practical option' for liberals quavering over the war. It is, they wrote, 'to begin immediately campaigning for a more ambitious, comprehensive and compassionate reconstruction of Iraq ... while supporting the war effort that will lay the groundwork for such plans to be enacted'.

Just and Penniman state two grounds for their claim to have identified the 'only moral and practical option'. The first is a call to consistency. Now that the war has started, they write, the liberation of Iraq from Saddam Hussein's regime is at hand. Liberals must support the rebuilding of Iraqi schools as much as they would the rebuilding of schools here at home.

In the second argument, as it turns out, morality and practicality are a matter of votes.

> Well, we have news for our progressive friends. Dread isn't going to fly with the majority of American voters – and it isn't progressive. In two months, US forces will have liberated Iraq from Hussein's rule. How will a temperament of permanent dread look then? Imagine the line George W. Bush will land over and over again on the campaign trail 'For those who said we couldn't plant the seed of democracy in the Middle East, I say, 'Never doubt the resolve of the American people.'

Is this, then, where liberals are? To have our views, our attitudes and our convictions – our very conception of morality – dictated, a full year in advance, by a prediction of a campaign slogan? Craven doesn't begin to describe it.

Just and Penniman's argument is based on a point of view widely held in advance of the war, and expressed on March 16 by Vice President Dick Cheney, who said: 'I really do believe that we will be greeted as liberators ... The read we get on the people of Iraq is there is no question but that they want to get rid of Saddam Hussein and they will welcome as liberators the United States when we come to do that.'

There is no need to doubt the sincerity of this view. Nor do we have, even now, decisive evidence to prove it entirely wrong. But, right or wrong, it has been proved irrelevant.

The fact remains that a very effective armed gang, numbering in the scores of thousands, presently governs Iraq. That gang will continue to offer stiff resistance first to occupation and later to reconstruction, until it is destroyed, root and branch, by a far superior force. And, as it is now clear, the application of that force, if it can succeed at all, must entail a horrific level of violence.

In planning for this war, the military professionals faced a choice. As many actually recommended, we could have built up a vast and over-whelming force and reduced Iraq to rubble from the air before moving in. Such a strategy was widely anticipated by anti-war forces world-wide; it formed the basis of many advance condemnations. However, it was correctly judged by our political leaders to be self-defeating politi-cally, in Iraq and in the wider world.

The other choice facing Secretary of Defense Donald Rumsfeld was to strike fast, with precision bombing ('shock and awe') and a fast-moving military force, bypassing the expected-to-be-friendly cities in the south and moving straight to Baghdad. But as strategy this entailed an elementary chess player's mistake: it did not take into account the reaction of the other side.

The main flaws are now plain. First, the strategy left very long supply lines exposed and vulnerable. Troops require water and tanks require gasoline. Without these, no force 250 miles from base will be useful for long. Second, Iraqi soldiers embedded in civilian populations – both those along supply lines and in Baghdad – can only be destroyed alongside those populations. Thus the Iraqis could force the transfor-mation of the second strategy into the first. And, being military real-ists, they have done so.

The dilemma is now acute. Retreat is unthinkable. George W. Bush's neoconservatives (standing safely in the back) will figuratively execute any who quail. The level of violence will therefore be raised. Mean-while, the prime stocks of precision munitions have been drawn down, and speculation about the use of cluster bombs and napalm and other vile weapons is being heard. And so the political battle – the battle for hearts and minds – will be lost. If history is a guide, you cannot subdue a large and hostile city except by destroying it completely. Short of massacre, we will not inherit a pacified Iraq.

For this reason, the project of reconstruction is impossible. No one should imagine that the civilians sent in to do this work can be made secure. To support 'the groundwork' for this effort is to support a holocaust, quite soon, against Iraqi civilians and also against the troops on both sides. That is what victory means. You can watch the beginnings (if you have satellite television) even now, as injured children fill up the hospitals of Baghdad.

The moral strategy would be to avoid the holocaust. To achieve that from the present disastrous position, the United States would have to accept a ceasefire, which would lead to the withdrawal of coalition forces under safe conduct. There would be no military dishonor in such a step. It would, however, entail the humiliation of the entire Bush Administration, indeed its well-deserved political collapse. Too bad the moral strategy is not a practical one.

The practical alternative? It is to oppose, to speak up and to write against the war, to expose and illuminate the frightful choices we confront. Let us remind our leaders at every turn of their recklessness and miscalculation. The American public may, if it chooses, reject the liberal position and support the hawks. But let us give them a choice. It is quite sure anyway that no one, in a situation as grave as this, will line up behind a platform of pre-emptive cringing.

(*The American Prospect* online, 1 April 2003. After publishing this piece, I wanted very badly to believe it was wrong. Unfortunately, it wasn't.)

Don't Blame Rumsfeld, Blame Bush

As the reality of this war sets in, the hunt for scapegoats is starting. Donald Rumsfeld finds himself described, by military and intelligence officers, as a 'businessman' whose 'micromanagement' has produced a 'stalemate', with the possibility of 'a political and military disaster'. For a war only ten days old, the back-biting is astounding. Still, Rumsfeld is the wrong man to blame.

The military men charge that Rumsfeld questioned every call-up, every proposal that the invasion be preceded by mass bombardment, every demand for the use of overwhelming force. Perhaps he did. But if so he was right to do it, for two reasons. The first is that smart generals are like labor leaders: they ask for more, knowing they will have to make do with less. And Rumsfeld, as a businessman, seems to have understood this very well.

Rumsfeld also knew that this war is a political war. To win it, to reconstruct Iraq, to fulfill the grand visions of Wolfowitz, Feith and Perle, to be in position to pressure Syria and Iran in the aftermath – all this required that the violence be kept down. 'Shock and awe' was designed to save Iraqi lives. The fast rush for Baghdad, bypassing the towns and cities on the supply routes, had the same intention and – initially – the same effect.

True enough, this strategy depended on the assumption that the Iraqis would not fight. More precisely, it assumed that major resistance would be limited to the regime's hard core, entrenched at Baghdad. Thus coalition forces could quickly assemble outside that city, stockpile supplies, and attack while they were fresh and before the weather got too hot.

The risk that the Iraqis would defend every town, harass the supply lines, bog down the Marines, prevent the quick occupation of Basra and Baghdad, even keep Umm Qasr unsecured for a week was not unknown. But the warnings were overruled – a serious, and potentially a disastrous mistake. Rumsfeld, however, is not responsible for that.

On May 16 Vice President Dick Cheney told the world, on *Meet the Press*:

> I really do believe that we will be greeted as liberators. I've talked with a lot of Iraqis in the last several months myself, had them to the White House. *The President* and I have met with them ... The read *we get* on the people of Iraq is there is no question but that they want to get rid of Saddam Hussein and they will welcome as liberators the United States when we come to do that. (Emphasis added)

The judgment that the Iraqis would not fight came from the White House. It came from the President. On this critical point, Rumsfeld was following orders.

Military history from Gallipoli to the Bay of Pigs is full of invasions that fail because politicians in the invading powers underrate the will to resist of a nation fighting with inferior weapons but greater numbers and on its own soil. And, as a group of German experts pointed out this week, military history also records no case of the successful invasion of a major hostile city. In World War II Leningrad and Stalingrad held out; Berlin fell only after it had been utterly destroyed.

It is the job of the President of the United States to know these things. It is the job of the Commander in Chief to ask hard questions about strategies laid before him, to evaluate risks, to spot the faulty assumptions underlying the grand plans.

But how can this be, when the President appoints himself (and on what experience?) as the nation's chief intelligence analyst?

John F. Kennedy refused to invade Laos in 1961 and Cuba in 1962. Lyndon B. Johnson refused to invade North Vietnam in 1967. George H.W. Bush refused to go to Baghdad in 1991. In each case, these leaders looked at the plans and judged the risks – military and diplomatic – to be too great.

Yet we know now that George W. Bush decided to attack Iraq before July 2002. Condoleezza Rice so informed Richard Haass, who has told Nicholas Lemann, who has reported it in the *New Yorker*. The decision came first and the planning later. And when the round peg of political necessity met the square hole of potential Iraqi defiance, Bush just got out his hammer and forced it in.

Now the military has to come up with Plan B: reinforcement, attrition, siege. Can this save the day? We'll see. And if not, the fault will belong to George Bush. In comparison, Donald Rumsfeld is a bit player.

(*The Texas Observer*, 30 April 2003)

The Iraqi Quagmire

Sergio Vieira de Mello was the real thing. I met him in East Timor in 2001, at the US mission on the evening of July 4, 2001. He told my brother (his colleague in the transition cabinet) that he would not attend a dinner for the Australian foreign minister that night: 'because I dislike him *intensely'*. Two days later I saw him again, as we joined the new East Timor self-defense forces for the last leg of a march to a new training ground. On that day, surrounded by guerrillas, their UN officers and the civilian staff, out on the road in the bright tropical sunshine, he was clearly having a good time.

Sergio was blunt, charming, energetic, funny. He knew his business, minced no words, commanded the loyalty of his mission and the respect of the Timorese. They knew he was working for *them* – for the cause of a free and independent and self-governing East Timor. And so it should have been in Iraq.

But it wasn't. We face in Iraq what the UN did not face in East Timor: an organized, brutal opposition, able to strike when and where it chooses. Why is this so? Partly because in Iraq large parts of the population do not want us there, and are prepared to abet those who would throw us out. The UN mission was simply an auxiliary target. And the security at the Canal Hotel was not good.

None of this should be surprising. Last November, at his request, I wrote a private memorandum to Gary Hart (a friend going back to the start of the McGovern effort in 1971) on how the situation might unfold. Here's what I said:

> while the impending war on Iraq may prove to be fairly easy ... the post-war occupation is certainly going to be ugly. Iraq is a huge country. The oil fields [and] the cities ... will need to be protected.

The protectors will need to be protected. Saddam has 150,000 secret police who will not physically disappear. There is a large Shi'a population with whom our relations could deteriorate quickly if their leaders don't like our rule. Worst of all there is Al Qaeda. They are not in Iraq right now, but they will be. And they will find plenty of fresh targets in occupied Iraq. Algeria comes to mind; does anyone remember?

... Saddam's government is ugly, but at present at least the Kurdish population is protected from him at low cost. The case for putting the U.S. Army at the service of the rest of the opposition remains totally unpersuasive and cannot be coherently made. This point becomes obvious when one reads the screeds suggesting that Iraq might somehow become an oasis of democracy in the Middle East. They are mostly written by people who fought to the last against a free vote for the presidency in Florida.

Once we have invaded, getting out again is not going to be easy. On the contrary, it will be very easy for Al Qaeda and others to guarantee just enough turmoil to ensure that it is *never* quite safe to leave. The choice will therefore become one of staying and bleeding, or of accepting an ignominious retreat – think the Israelis from South Lebanon but on a much larger scale. People need to understand that a decision to invade Iraq is, in effect, a decision to establish what will be, for practical purposes, a *permanent* zone of occupation there ...

Empire is an economic system. But it is a system that works only in the presence of an overwhelming advantage of force, a general acquiescence of the regional leadership, large local security forces, and an absence of determined opposition. The British held India because, and only so long as, they enjoyed these advantages. In the Sudan, the matter was already different as early as the 1880s. The final outcome against the Mahdists at Omdurman was as it was only because, as Hilaire Belloc put it: 'Whatever happens, we have got/The Maxim Gun, and they have not.'

But in modern conditions the correlation of forces does not lie with the imperial power. Explosives, mines, booby traps, rockets and similar weapons of resistance are too cheap and too effective. We will certainly face determined opposition in Iraq, sooner or later and possibly sooner, once the euphoria following the overthrow of Saddam wears off and as our other enemies get a chance to get into the game. The same will be increasingly true of our position elsewhere in the Middle East. In the face of determined opposition, empire has costs that no modern democracy can sustain – and certainly not the United States with our attachment to peacetime prosperity and abhorrence of body bags.

What happened to Sergio Vieira de Mello, to his dedicated colleagues at the United Nations mission in Baghdad, what has been happening to American soldiers and to innocent Iraqi civilians every single day, was terribly easy to predict. And the result? A UN staffer put it very well: 'We send our best guy to Iraq and he comes home in a box.'

Note

Sergio Vieira de Mello, the United Nations Special Representative in Iraq, was killed in a truck bombing of the UN headquarters in Baghdad, 19 August 2003.

(*The Texas Observer*, 29 August 2003)

War and Economy Don't Wear Well

On both jobs and Iraq, the good news Bush tells us is contradicted by the bad news that we feel in our bones.

In Iraq, things seem fine in the far north, stable enough in the south. But the Sunni triangle is trouble. Occupation is expensive, resistance is cheap. Soft targets emerge quickly in any reconstruction effort. 'Improvised explosive devices' work against hotels, police stations, pipelines and jeeps on patrol. Soldiers are not police. Civil order can be maintained only through the cooperation of civilians or by terror. For us the entire game depends on whether the civil population wants us to succeed more than they fear our opponents.

Will the Iraqi people rally, in time? They need reasons. To me, the Bremer economic plan looks disastrous: a 'Morgenthau Plan' to de-industrialize Iraq masquerading as a Marshall Plan to rebuild it. Accounts of corruption and inefficiency are not reassuring. Another reported problem is that Republican Party policy hacks have been dumped on Iraq, unsupervised. And so, the occupation has been making economic decisions with reckless disregard for local sentiment. This will alienate the very public opinion on which any hope for security relies.

It is too early to call it quits. But we should set some clear targets. By next summer, either there will be security or there won't be. The electricity and water will be fixed, or not. Oil will be flowing, or it won't be. And Iraqis will be down the road toward their own government – with the right to determine how their own economy works – or they won't be. If there is sharp improvement, the soldiers will be on their way home anyway, and Bush will then be able to say, 'mission accomplished after all'. Otherwise, it will be fair to judge. Absent real progress this winter and next spring, there will be no reason to give Bush or Bremer more time.

The other turnaround issue is our economy. Here the 'invasion force' is the power of war spending and the 'improvised explosive device' is the consumer debt bomb. War spending doubled the growth rate earlier this year. In the third quarter, consumers jumped on board, business investment finally picked up, and the growth rate doubled again.

If this continues, real recovery, with growth rapid enough to add jobs, might just come next year. The possibility can't be ruled out. Cars and computers are getting old. Prolonged low interest rates must have brought down total debt service, creating some breathing room for new loans. And the Fed will keep rates low next year, giving Bush as much help as it can.

I still think it won't work. The economic growth rate needs to stay high for the year in order to bring unemployment down. Much of the spending we just saw came directly from the tax rebates, and they're gone now. Consumers may have been jumping on low interest rates for fear they would not last. If from now on they are even just a wee bit sensitive to their financial condition, or a little bit nervous about their jobs, or just a bit anxious about their retirements, or a wee bit worried about medical costs, or about rising tuition for their kids – they'll keep their money in the bank, for now.

In that case, growth will slow in the coming quarters, before picking up for one more false dawn before the election. That should come next spring, when tax refunds and the echo effect of the Iraq war – due to restocking of military equipment – have their impact. There may be some job creation, but Bush and company will still end up with the worst record on jobs since Hoover. Whether this will matter to the voters in the face of feelgood headlines is something we will just have to see.

For a moment, though, let's talk about the economy, and not just as an election issue. What will happen after the election, if Bush wins? Answer: he won't lead us back to full employment, even then. For two reasons.

First, full employment prosperity would require much, much more business investment. We got that in 1998–2000 in a wave of focused euphoria over technology. Some of it was real and some imagined, but we were all caught up in it, every day, and for this reason the money flowed. Remember? Can you imagine anything similar happening with a war on? I can't. Those daily pictures of burning Hummers have a bad effect on mood. Indeed this could be, in the end, the largest *economic* cost of Bush's war.

The second reason is that Bush doesn't *want* full employment. Why should he? His Administration is full of oil men, military contractors, mining and timber interests, big pharmaceuticals, big media and the like. Their interest is in market power, patents, government contracts. They aren't bothered by weak sales. And so, full employment doesn't matter to them, as it does to small business, retailers, and working people.

Even Republicans can run a boomlet for a while. But if the American people really want full employment prosperity on a sustained basis, they will have to vote for it, one year from now.

(*Newsday*, 4 November 2003)

How You Will Pay for the War

Well, it may be that the laws of economics remain in force. And one of them says: war causes inflation.

Every major war in the past century brought inflation to some degree. And so did two upheavals in the Middle East, the Yom Kippur War of 1973 and the Iranian Revolution of 1979, which did not directly involve the United States, except through their effect on the price of oil. Why is this so? The big reason is that wars must be paid for, somehow. They require resources that civilians would otherwise use. Those resources must be diverted to the war effort. Usually, inflation is the easiest way. World War I was largely financed by inflation, and so were the revolutionary and civil wars before that. So, though on a smaller scale, was Vietnam.

Inflation applies the law of the jungle to war finance. Prices and profits rise, wages and their purchasing power fall. Thugs, profiteers and the well-connected get rich. Working people and the poor make out as they can. Savings erode, through the unseen mechanism of the 'inflation tax' – meaning that the government runs a big deficit in nominal terms, but a smaller one when inflation is factored in. GNP rises with the national debt, but living standards do not.

Are we seeing the start of this once again? It is too early to tell for sure. At only about I percent of GDP, the Iraq war remains small so far. (However, one might add another percent or so for military spending increases not directly related to Iraq. Notably, these include President Bush's ballistic missile defense – militarily useless but sure to absorb construction materials in a tight market.)

In March, the Consumer Price Index hit 7.4 percent at an annual rate, up from only 1.4 percent over the previous year. No doubt there will be ups and downs in the months ahead. But one may well fear that a general trend toward higher inflation lies ahead. And this is true even if (as seems likely) there is no general wartime boom. That is partly because in a global economy even small price effects can be magnified in several ways, some of which we are now seeing. Here's why.

First, oil and gas prices – fundamental prices in our economy – are already high and still likely to rise. With gasoline averaging $1.80 per gallon around the country and hitting $2.49 at the hottest spots, transportation costs for all commodities are rising too. With oil at $37 per barrel – up $10 in the past six months – fertilizer and therefore food costs will be affected in the months ahead. Yes, as Bob Woodward reports in his new book, *Plan of Attack*, the Saudis may try to rescue Bush by cutting prices this summer – a feelgood gesture. And after the election, what do you think will happen?

Next, we find that inflation is breaking out in China – a consequence of that country's boom and rising demand for oil, steel and other commodities it must purchase on the global market. There will be pass-through to the price of Chinese imports to the United States. So there goes the major brake on inflation in the prices of our manufactured goods, something American consumers have benefited from for many years.

Then we will feel the effects of the dollar's decline on the prices of goods from Europe, Japan and Canada. The dollar's decline is already, no doubt, a component of the rising dollar price of oil. And this fact ensures that Europe suffers less than we do from the consequences of our occupation of Iraq. Markets reward the peaceable, as nations from Switzerland to Sweden to China have long known. Economically speaking, empire is a suckers' game.

And there is profiteering. Firms with monopoly power usually keep some in reserve. In wartime, if the climate is permissive, they bring it out and use it. Gas prices can go up when refining capacity becomes short – due partly to too many mergers. More generally, when sales to consumers are slow, businesses ought to cut prices – but many of them don't. Instead, they *raise* prices to meet their income targets and hope that the market won't collapse. Own a telephone? Cable TV? Electrical connection? Been to a doctor? Filled a prescription? Have a kid in college? Then you know what I mean.

Meanwhile, lurking in the background are Alan Greenspan and the Federal Reserve. They await the election and their moment to raise interest rates. The pressure is clearly building – as reflected in the hortatory tone of the *New York Times* headline on Floyd Norris's story on April 16: 'It's Time for an End to Super Low Interest Rates'.

Really? Says who? The theory that higher interest rates control inflation is based on the idea that inflation is driven by too much *civilian* spending, by too much business investment, and especially by greedy workers demanding big raises. But business investment has barely started to recover. Wages are not rising these days – how could they be? Real wages (adjusted for the price increases) are *falling*. Higher interest rates will add another injury to that one.

Think through what will actually happen when interest rates rise. For firms that administer prices, interest rates are just another cost. Like the rise in oil, the rise in rates will be passed through. Prices will rise. High interest rates may, indeed, choke off inflation eventually. But they do it in only one way: by forcing households and businesses to cut back, by squeezing people with debts, and therefore by slowing down the civilian economy. Expect this cure to come later, cheered on by the business press. It will be worse than the disease.

Higher interest rates, in other words, are not a way to fight inflation in the short run. They are, instead, part and parcel of the strategy of inflationary war finance. Their function is to help ensure that debtors pay, and creditors do not.

Is there another way? The answer is yes, but it isn't easy. In wars past – notably in World War II and Korea – the job was done by steeply progressive taxes including taxes on excess profits, by 'forced saving' (which was an essentially compulsory private holding of public debt), and by price control. Interest rates were frozen at 2 percent on government bonds – and essentially at zero on bank deposits. The principle was: no one profits from the war.

This combination kept inflation down – prices were stable from 1942 through 1945. Not many grew rich off that war. Instead, my generation grew up with series EE bonds to our names. They were the promise that those working to win the war would see some of the material fruits of their labor later, when peacetime production returned. Together with progressive taxes and stable prices, they formed a bond between those leading the war effort, and those working to support it.

It's clear that we shouldn't expect anything of the kind from Team Bush.

(*Salon*, 20 April 2004)

The Economics of the Oil War

Underlying the talk of weapons of mass destruction, democracy, human rights, and George W. Bush's supposed quest for personal vengeance against Saddam Hussein ('He tried to kill my Dad'). there has always lurked the suspicion that it was about oil. That maps of the Iraqi oil fields made their way to the Cheney energy task force back in 2001 doesn't exactly ease this suspicion. Neither does Bush's determination to stay in Iraq, now that vengeance is his – but the occupation is plainly failing to achieve any of its other objectives.

But if it was about oil, what exactly was the idea?

You might have thought that the purpose was to keep the price of oil low. The great American consumer likes low gas prices. The less-than-great American politician has generally known how to oblige – at least when elections loom. This is a non-partisan comment: as recently as 2000, let's recall, Clinton warded off an oil price spike, innocuously, by selling from the strategic reserve. There was talk, before the war, about doubling the output of the Iraqi oil regions. Ha! If low gas prices were a goal of this war, it isn't happening when it matters.

Instead, oil prices are soaring. And gasoline is up 18 cents since last year, to nearly $1.80 per gallon on average, with spikes as high as $2.49 in some places.

Immediate causes are said to include jitters over our hold on Iraq and surging Chinese demand. But another, surely, is the fall of the international dollar. As the dollar weakens against the euro, the dollar oil price must rise or the euro price will fall. We have, in short, a move toward de facto pricing of oil in euros. This is not a good sign for us.

Control of the oil fields is a burden for which we are spilling blood and treasure. But what do we get for it? The oil goes anyway on the world market, and the bidder with the strongest currency gets the best price. As we weaken our economy to control the oil at the source, the benefit of our imperial effort goes elsewhere – to those who do not pay. Back in the sixteenth century, Philip II of Spain tried the same thing in Mexico and Peru, with a similar result. (Indeed, Keynes once calculated that the entire net asset position of the British Empire in 1914 could be traced back to the booty of the Golden Hind, plus compound interest.)

Empire, in other words, is a suckers' game.

Is it possible that Bush went into Iraq to raise the price of oil? Bush has attacked Kerry, of course, for having once voted for a fifty-cent gas tax. And in the wake, some old Cheney quotes favoring high energy prices for the United States quickly surfaced. US domestic oil producers have high costs. That an old oilman like Cheney likes high prices is no very big surprise.

But this argument has two problems. First, high oil prices can bring on economic recession, lowering demand and defeating their own purpose. (Treasury Secretary John Snow warned on this point this week, and he was probably not blowing smoke.) Second, if you really wanted to get the gas price up there were easier ways to do it than by occupation of Iraq. Bush has friends in Saudi Arabia, after all.

That brings us to a third possibility. Was it all about the companies who would control and exploit the Iraqi reserves? Granted, it makes no material difference to you or me whether Phillips or, say, Yukos pumps the oil from around Basra or Kirkuk. But to those companies, it matters a lot. New reserves are hard to find these days – and an oil company without reserves doesn't have much of a future. Needless to say, the contracts to run the fields are also the lifeblood of firms like Halliburton and Bechtel.

Could that be it? Did Dick Cheney take us into war in Iraq just for the sake of market share for his friends? At the cost of 500 US combat dead so far, some 14,000 wounded, and tens of thousand dead and injured Iraqis? At the budget cost, paid by you and me, of roughly one hundred billion dollars every year? It seems difficult to believe. And I don't believe it, on the evidence so far. But I'd like to know for sure. What were those maps about? Unless someone talks, or spills the papers, we may never know.

And then there is a fourth possibility. An elaborate thesis holds that we went into Iraq not so much to get the oil there as to stabilize the situation in Saudi Arabia. Our troops there (since the first Gulf War) were a problem – a problem that partly led to 9/11 and that also threatened the House of Saud. We needed a new base. Iraq would be it. As Jay Garner candidly put it, Iraq would be our Philippines: a coaling station for the century ahead. From there, in particular, we could support the Saudis without causing them undue trouble at home.

This theory is just crazy enough, and the logic behind it just stupid enough, to be possible. The stability of Saudi Arabia, sad to say, is an ugly problem. But the solution? Too bad people forgot that we massacred hundreds of thousands to control the Philippines, at a time when the world was much more forgiving of mass murder than it is today.

And so, are you enjoying the price of gas? Better get used to it. Until we deal with our energy problem with sensible diversification, conservation and innovation – you'll be paying a price in both treasure and blood, for a long time.

(Previously unpublished, 2004)

Boom Times for War Inc.

On September 21, 2001, the American Stock Exchange created the Amex Defense Index, a measure of the stock prices of fifteen corporations who together account for about 80 percent of procurement and research contracting by the Department of Defense. The index of course includes the five largest contractors: Lockheed Martin, Boeing, Raytheon, Northrop Grumman and General Dynamics.

The chart below, published in a new paper by economists Luc Mampaey and Claude Serfati, shows what has happened since then. With the Afghan war the arms index surged, gaining over 25 percent by April 2002. Then it slumped, along with the rest of the market. If

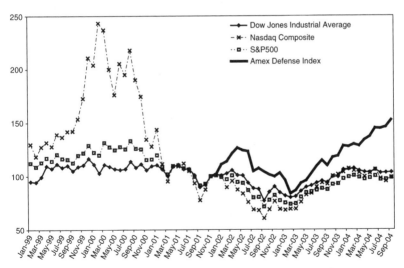

Figure 3   The American stock exchange and the Amex Defense Index

you had invested a thousand dollars in a defense portfolio at the peak of the Taliban boomlet, by March 2003 you would have lost a third of your stake.

But then came Iraq. And it's been clover for contractors ever since. Total gains since March 2003 are above 80 percent. And even if you'd put your money in at the beginning, in September of 2001, you're up over 50 percent. That isn't bad, considering.

This is no scandal, of course. War is naturally good for the arms business. The companies are public: anyone can buy their stocks. Suppose that (back in 2001) you'd had unlimited access to bank credit. And suppose you'd also had the certain knowledge that George W. Bush would take out Saddam Hussein, come what may. Well then, you too could have made billions over the past three years.

And if you were the Carlyle Group, to which ex-President George Herbert Walker Bush then served as a senior adviser – and which was meeting at the Ritz-Carlton Hotel in Washington DC on the morning of September 11, 2001? Well, in that case, you did very well indeed. The Carlyle Group today describes itself as 'the leading private equity investor in the aerospace and defense industries'. There is no reason to doubt that claim.

The really big scandal lies elsewhere. It isn't in the fact that a small group of political insiders made big money from the Iraq war. The big scandal is in all those other numbers. The Dow Jones Industrial Average. The Standard and Poor's 500. The NASDAQ Composite Index. Look at them. They haven't budged in three years.

Some people see problems when the stock market goes up. They fret over bubbles (which must pop) and over the inequality of wealth that naturally rises with a rising market, given that only a few Americans own most of the corporate stock. These are real problems. But count me in the group that tends to see the bright side. A rising stock market means that businesses are seeing the possibilities of future profit. This spurs their decisions to invest. And that, above all, is what creates the new jobs so lacking in the past four years.

And so, if you want a one-picture analysis of the American Economic Problem, this graph is as good as any you will ever find. It exposes with brutal clarity the Bush economy as it really is – run for the profit of the President's friends. And the graph exposes with equal clarity the largest economic cost of the Iraq war. That's the blockade the war has laid across and against the full recovery of everyone else.

Much has been made, of course, of the fact that Bush's tax cuts went overwhelmingly to the top 1 percent of the income distribution. But if those tax cuts had succeeded in setting off a strong and widespread economic expansion – as Ronald Reagan's did, twenty years ago – who would care? Not me, frankly. The problem is that they failed to do this. Part of the reason lies in the poor design of those cuts. And part, almost surely, lies in the fact that the Iraq war stands as a huge question mark across the future of the American economy, and hence a deterrent to business investment.

Business isn't stupid. It knows that Iraq took us away from the 'War on Terror'. It knows we're less safe now than if we'd pursued Al Qaeda to the bitter end. It knows that energy markets are unsettled, and that we may be heading toward a long period of expensive oil. It knows, perhaps above all, that the war in Iraq is far from over. And it knows that certain Washington insiders are even now busily preparing for a post-election showdown with Iran. None of this is likely to inspire confidence.

Back in 1919, in the wake of the Great War, John Maynard Keynes wrote of the effects of war on business. 'The war has disclosed,' he wrote, 'the possibility of consumption to all and the vanity of abstinence to many.' Something like this happened after September 2001. Households borrowed and kept up their spending even as incomes shrank. But businesses, forward-looking and unsettled by the prospects ahead, curtailed investment. As Keynes also wrote, 'no longer confident of the future, [they] seek to enjoy more fully their liberties of consumption so long as they last'. But they don't invest. And they don't create jobs.

The big scandal isn't who made money. It's who didn't. It isn't the handful who got good jobs working for defense firms. (It isn't the brave truck drivers risking their lives on the roads of Iraq.) It's the millions who got nothing at all. It's the fact that George W. Bush did nothing about it. Message, once again: Bush doesn't care.

And so the lines between the two great issues of this campaign – the jobless economy and the Iraq war – are blurred. The economy is part of the price we are paying for the war.

And on both, the Bush message is the same: Things Are Fine. The Economy Is Strong and Getting Stronger. Baghdad is Safe and Getting Safer. And The Infidel is Being Thrown Into the Sea.

Oh, excuse me. The last one isn't Bush. It's from Baghdad Bob – Comical Ali – Saddam Hussein's minister of information, as Bill Maher brilliantly reminded us the other day.

Let Bush join him in quiet retirement in Dubai.

(*Salon*, 30 September 2004)

The Gambler's Fallacy

> You can't win and you can't break even; you can't get out of
> the game.

Iraq is a war of occupation. A striking fact about wars of occupation is
that while they were often successful until around the end of World
War II, they have seldom succeeded in the years since. Up until then
occupations, also called empires, were routine. Today, they are rare.
What changed about the world to make this so? Here are six things:

- First, there is urbanization. A dispersed rural population is much
  easer to control than a packed-in urban middle class. This is partly
  architecture: cityscapes favor the defender; so the Germans learned
  at Stalingrad and it isn't going to change.
- Second, there is the correlation of force. Around 1898 Hilaire Belloc
  immortally wrote, 'Whatever happens, we have got/The Maxim Gun.
  And they have not'. Now the booby trap, the car bomb, and the suicide
  attacker give the occupied simple but effective weapons. They impose
  a focus on force protection that gets in the way of everything else.
- Third, imperialists governed through local rulers; today, people
  everywhere expect sovereignty. The insurgency is effective in central
  Iraq in part because government there isn't yet truly sovereign.
  People may dislike it, or perhaps they merely fear it will fail. Either
  way, we are denied the most important instrument of governance,
  the cooperation of the governed.
- Fourth, well into the twentieth century, terror and torture were
  accepted features of occupation. The British killed 20,000 in Iraq in
  the early 1920s and few complained. Earlier the Belgians killed some
  ten million in the Congo; almost no one knew. In the 1870s we
  drove the Plains Indians toward extermination. But since Algeria,
  since Vietnam, television has radically raised the visibility of violence, and the associated political price.

- Fifth, today war marches with the free market. When our troops went in, Iraq lost control of its frontiers. Imported cars clogged the streets; it has become easy for insurgents to move with concealed bombs. Meanwhile a flood of electrical appliances drains the power grid, however much new capacity is added. Subsidized fuel is easily exported, so fuel is short. (Yet if subsidies are reduced or eliminated, tolerance for the occupation falls.) Not to mention that imports destroy local jobs, creating a pool of frustrated unemployed.
- Sixth, there is the fact that an army of occupation nowadays is a rotating force. Soldiers come and go. This is necessary for the survival of a volunteer army. But it is corrosive to stable intelligence relationships in the theater of operations; every new rotation of forces must relearn local conditions and rebuild relations of trust.

These are facts that one has to deal with, and the question is this: is there a strategy that can deal with them under the present circumstances in Iraq?

The answer can only lie with Iraqi self-government. It lies in the development by that government of an effective permanent Iraqi national security force. This is obvious to everyone. But will this government be able to muster a capable army and an effective police? And if so, in how much time? Are we in position to set a realistic deadline to finish the job?

That's a hard question. Previous timetables – for sovereignty, for the elections – were apparently quite effective in motivating decisions and action. Perhaps a timetable for Iraqi takeover of internal security – say one year following the next elections, so December 2006, would be equally so.

But a timetable might also hurt, as Bush argues. It could cause the collapse of existing intelligence channels on insurgent activity (if we have any of value). And a timetable for our withdrawal might also become a timetable for the de facto independence of Kurdistan, implying eventual Kurdish withdrawal from the new Iraqi army. The question is whether, without the Kurds, Shiite Arabs alone can possibly construct an effective counter-insurgent force.

Effective against whom? Unfortunately, it now seems clear we are not actually fighting merely a loose confederation of remnants, dead-enders, criminals and jihadis. The 'insurgency' is at its heart the work of Saddam Hussein's internal security forces, the armed gang that governed Iraq for 35 years. And it is pursuing a campaign planned, equipped and financed well in advance of our invasion. That's a tough opponent. And while it can't beat us, there is no evidence yet that we can defeat it, either.

And if that's so, what is our real choice? Is it between a war continuing for twenty years, with a thousand or so American dead every year and no assurance of success, and on the other side of the coin the return of the Baath? If that is the choice, which alternative would you pick? And if you set a timetable in order to discover the truth – something that in spite of the horrific character of this dilemma may still be a sensible idea – what do you do if the timetable fails?

I have no answer to that question. Here's my view. *Morally*, we are committed to protecting the Iraqi Arabs from the return of their old tormentors. (The Kurds, mercifully, can protect themselves in their own homeland.) *Ideally*, we'd like a military victory – not too bloody – followed by a political reconciliation in the Arab areas of Iraq. *Practically*, the pursuit of that goal will probably cost us our present deployment, and present rate of losses, for the indefinite future. And the *best result* will be a weak, theocratic Shiite government in Arab Iraq, with no effective army, rendered unstable indefinitely by Sunni Arab opposition.

Indeed there may be no way to prevent a cataclysmic ending, except by staying in place indefinitely. And that raises a question. *Do we have an obligation to stay indefinitely, merely to keep those who have cooperated with us alive?*

That's a pretty good question for those who chose this war. Yet at another level, the rest of us can't escape posing it for ourselves. We're still implicated in what happens next. And we should not make the mistake of the neocons, to assume the best for the policy we'd like to see.

For this reason, all who advocate withdrawal from Iraq should be very careful. The practical correctness of the antiwar position – now revealed – does not establish that withdrawal is workable today. It's true that *we* would never have launched this war. It's true that no compelling national interest requires an indefinite US presence in Iraq. But are we free to leave? Not until the potential for a true catastrophe on our exit is contained. For all we know, that may not be the case for decades.

The point being, maybe we're stuck. And if so, will this teach us anything – finally – about the usefulness of diplomacy, the value of patience, and the need for the most extreme caution in using US military force, and about the people now in power? The President in Brussels stated that our basic values were a 'vibrant opposition, a free press, shared power and the rule of law'. Could we start behaving in *this* country as though that were true? Will this happen in time to change the balance of the debate *over Syria, and Iran*? Let's hope so. For real security will elude us all, so long as reckless men and women can stampede the country into reckless wars.

Note

These comments are condensed from remarks prepared for the Security Policy Working Group forum on exit strategies from Iraq, Washington, DC, 22 February 2005. It was based on remarks delivered to a leadership symposium of the Army V Corps in Heidelberg, Germany, earlier that month, at the request of commanding general Ricardo Sanchez.

Withdrawal Symptoms

In November 2004, Lt General Ricardo Sanchez came to a luncheon at my professional home, the LBJ School of Public Affairs. I attended and asked some inconvenient questions. It was an inconsequential exchange, but two weeks later I received a surprising invitation. Would I fly to Germany in February and speak to the leadership of the Army V Corps about the operational conditions of Iraq? I have no military experience, and have never been to Iraq, while many in my audience – mostly generals and colonels – had spent over a year there. But of course I went. My unstated assignment was to say some inconvenient things, which may have otherwise gone unsaid.

Inconvenience has since gone public, big time. Back in November, Representative John Murtha (D-Pa) gave a breakthrough speech, describing the troops as 'stretched thin': 'Recruitment is down, even as our military has lowered its standards. Defense budgets are being cut. Personnel costs are skyrocketing ... Choices will have to be made.' At the same time, Murtha added, success in Iraq is very remote.

> Oil production and energy production are below pre-war levels. Our reconstruction efforts have been crippled by the security situation. Only $9 billion of the $18 billion appropriated for reconstruction has been spent. Unemployment remains at about 60 percent. Clean water is scarce ... And most importantly, insurgent incidents have increased from about 150 per week to over 700 in the last year ... Since the revelations at Abu Ghraib, American casualties have doubled.

For this, Cheney blasted him, but then it emerged that Murtha's crime was tipping the Administration's own hand. It appears we are beginning a long, slow, painful retreat from Iraq.

But are we drawing the full and correct lessons from this disaster? Some former liberal hawks now take refuge in what Sam Rosenfeld and Matthew Yglesias call 'the incompetence dodge': that things would have turned out okay if only the neocon cabal were not in charge. Such libhawks would withdraw US forces only to use them again, in another (but, of course, more justified and better planned) war. And that would mean a bigger war, with a bigger force on the ground, and a much bigger budget to support it.

But the reality is that the Iraq war could not be won by a force of any size or by an expenditure of any amount. Against determined opposition, occupations in the modern world cannot prevail. They haven't for more than 60 years. The reason is that the basic economics of warfare have changed. Here are six reasons I gave to the officers in Germany – a pure exercise in stating what they already knew.

Sixty years ago the then-colonial world was mostly rural; today it consists of enormous cities. These urban jungles of concrete provide vast advantages – concealment, fortification, communication, intelligence – to the defender. In cities, troops on patrol are isolated and exposed; their location is always known, while that of the enemy is not. More patrols mean more targets. The superior firepower of the occupiers just means that a lot more innocent people get hurt.

So does the 'crude' weaponry of insurgents. Car bombs, booby traps, and suicide belts are cheap and effective. Detonated by radio or wire from within a nearby building, roadside bombs equalize the insurgent and the invader. Detonated by fanatics, suicide bombs are extremely difficult to stop. Shaped explosives, which have started to appear in Iraq, are able to burn right through armor plate. To prevent these attacks means emphasizing force protection; this gets in the way of everything else.

The violence in Iraq is horrific, but it's the media that makes it intolerable. Indeed, the violence is horrific only by modern standards. To truly cow a colonial population (as in British India in 1857, or on the American plains in the late nineteenth century) requires mass murder on a far larger scale. The presence of the media makes this most inconvenient. As we demonstrated at Fallujah, the sure way to subdue a hostile city is to destroy it. But that's no way to win a political war back home – or hearts and minds in Iraq.

Jet travel is a military mixed blessing. Today's army works on rotations; soldiers are deployed for about a year and then (in principle at least) they come home. When that happens, local liaisons and intelligence relationships must be rebuilt. On the other hand, if soldiers are denied the right to rotate home, their morale is going to suffer far more than in the old days when there was no such expectation. Email and blogs make sure that morale problems get home fast when the soldiers do not.

As if that were not enough, war today cannot escape the free market. When we invaded Iraq, the borders collapsed and import restrictions were eliminated. Imports surged, notably of electrical appliances like air conditioners and refrigerators. By the time the electricity supply was rebuilt, demand had skyrocketed, and the power could run for only a few hours a day. Without control over electrical demand, the reconstruction effort was crippled, and the Americans couldn't win the Iraqi people's respect and support. They were expecting miracles, after all, and they didn't get them.

Finally, there has been a fundamental change of expectations: call it the presumption of independence. The British may have believed that their empire would always be the 'dread and envy of them all', but today no one believes the American presence in Iraq can endure over the long term. So unless you are in a safe zone (like Kurdistan) or part of an exiled elite with a posh flat in London, it does not pay to cuddle up to the occupying power. The retribution could be most unpleasant.

These are now the fundamental facts of wars of occupation. They tell us that foreign military power cannot long prevail over the territory of a people – in this case, the Sunnis of central Iraq – who are prepared to resist it to the death. This does not necessarily mean that the new Iraq will collapse when we leave. But if we cannot defeat the insurgency, then the insurgents will have to be accommodated, somehow, politically. Or else we leave the country to fight it out even more brutally in our absence.

We should have known we'd face this situation. In tiny East Timor, a ragtag band of resisters harried the Indonesian army for more than 25 years; that band (splendid people, by the way) now runs the world's newest independent state. In Afghanistan, US-assisted guerrillas drove out the Red army; their successors now make most of the country ungovernable. In Chechnya, the country has been destroyed but the rebellion hasn't been subdued. And then there was Vietnam.

During the Cold War, we ringed the world with bases – but always in alliance with existing governments that were legitimate, at least up to a point. One may disapprove of the regimes we supported, but this model for the projection of military power works. It is called 'containment'. It works as long as the host regimes remain viable and as long as the military power it projects isn't tested in actual combat. When these conditions failed – in Iran, in the Philippines, in Vietnam – so did the strategy.

The successful use of military power – as Mao Zedong understood when he called America a 'paper tiger' – entails a large element of bluff. Vietnam deflated the image that American power could never be challenged. To some extent, the Gulf War of 1991 restored that image, but the restoration was achieved by the limited aims and quick termination of that war. The Clinton successes in the Balkans came in part because all sides bought this lesson of the Gulf War. (With Serbia, the bluff came close to being called again; the Kosovo bombing campaign took 80 days and Russian diplomacy rescued us in the end.)

But now Iraq has once again exposed what military power cannot achieve, short of nuclear weapons. Iran and North Korea have taken notice. Meanwhile, our friends, the Europeans and the Japanese, must be asking themselves: exactly what sort of security does the American alliance buy, and at what price?

Bush and Cheney have done more than merely bungle a war and damage the Army. They have destroyed the foundation of the post-Cold War world security system, which was the accepted authority of American military power. That reputation is now gone. It cannot be restored simply by retreating from Iraq. This does not mean that every ongoing alliance will now collapse. But they are all more vulnerable than they were before, and once we leave central Iraq, they will be weaker still. As these paper tigers start to blow in the wind, so too will America's economic security erode.

From this point of view, the fuss over whether we were misled into war – is the sky blue? Is the grass green? – stands in the way of a deeper debate that should start quite soon and ask this question: now that Bush and Cheney have screwed up the only successful known model for world security under our leadership, what the devil do we do?

(*Mother Jones*, March–April 2006)

About Greenspan

Back to the Cross of Gold

One thing my old Yale classmate Jaime Serra Puche and I have in common, besides our names, is that we're both entitled to be sore at Alan Greenspan.

Financially, I'm a simple case. I have an Adjustable Rate Mortgage, tied to a short-term interest rate, which now costs me about $2000 per year more than it did a year ago. I have some savings in a pension fund, partly in stocks and bonds that have lost value this year. I have an income, too, but that hasn't changed. You get the picture.

Jaime's case is also simple. He has a country, called Mexico, that has been borrowing, at an adjustable rate, to finance roads, schools, water and power systems. He has an investment, called the peso, now worth 30 percent less than it was just last month. Oh, and Jaime doesn't have an income. Until a few days ago he was Finance Minister. Now he's unemployed.

There are lots more like us – not to be hurt when interest rates rise you have to be very rich, quite poor, or a hermit. Even being rich doesn't always do it. Orange County, California, one of the richest places on earth, borrowed short to invest long, got caught in the squeeze and went bankrupt. Or consider Uncle Sam himself, who cut $500 billion from his five-year deficit in 1993, only to have $150 billion or more added back in new five-year interest costs when rates rose. (In 1993, Uncle Sam also cut back on his long-term borrowing in favor of short-term bills, to take advantage of those low short-term interest rates that then didn't stay low. Tough luck, taxpayers.)

Speaking of bankrupts, the chief political victims of all this are President Clinton and the Democratic Party. They were the ones who promised, back in 1992, that we would be better off by now. Some of us are: employment is up, thank you, and profits are up by over a third. But most of us aren't better off: average wages haven't risen one bit in two years and wages are what most of us earn. Low interest rates were supposed to make up for this, to be the great benefit of deficit reduction, or so we were told. Remember? It might have worked too, if interest rates had stayed down. But they didn't.

It would be nice to think that in raising rates, Alan Greenspan and the Federal Reserve Board were serving some higher public purpose – such as fighting inflation. But no. Greenspan and company haven't offered any serious argument that raising rates was necessary to fight off inflation. Inflation was low before rates started rising, remains low today, was and is forecast to remain low in the future. Except for the fact that deficit reduction passed, circumstances did not change between 1993 and 1994. And that change should have brought stable rates, not increases. It was a bait-and-switch, pure and simple.

Greenspan and company wanted, among other things, to scare middle income folks out of stock and bond mutual funds and back into liquid assets (like money market funds and, you guessed it, bank deposits) – for the benefit of our friends the commercial bankers. Greenspan actually said this, more or less, to the Senate Banking Committee last May (I was there and heard him). But only recently has the watchdog press woken up. The *New York Times* had a piece in December charting the rise in rates and the fall in the stock market. Guess what? Week by week, they track pretty well.

Why then aren't interest rates a political issue? One reason is that we seem to lack a political leader with the nerve to make them one. The President won't do it. Newt Gingrich, for his part, actually did say that he thought high interest rates were a problem. But someone got to him quickly, and he retracted. As H.L. Mencken once cracked about some surgery on Randolph Churchill: 'the doctors found the one part of his body that was *not* malignant, and removed it'.

Cutting middle-class taxes is now the agenda – to be paid for, in Clinton's proposal, by cuts in public housing for the poor and in trans-portation spending. (Thanks, but at that price I'll pass on my share.) The Republicans are, as ever, worse but more authentic: they'll cut capital gains taxes for the rich, add another $12 billion or so to the military, and take it all out of welfare.

The points to remember here are (1) yes, Virginia, the Federal Reserve really does control the (short-term) rate of interest; (2) the point of deficit reduction in 1993 and now of 'paying' for tax cuts by screwing the poor was supposedly to raise (or maintain) 'national savings' and so to drive down the (long-term) rate of interest, thereby stimulating investment and productivity growth; and (3) the Federal Reserve has spoiled that game, by driving up the short-term rate until the effects spill over into long-term markets and the benefits of deficit reduction (if any) are lost.

So why bother with holding the deficit down?

The true Democrats might begin their comeback by proposing to cut working-class taxes big-time, say by knocking two full points off the social security payroll tax and thereby eliminating the *surplus* in those funds, which presently is not used for social security but is rather lent back to the rest of the government and spent on everything else the government does. If doing this means breaking the budget rules, well then, break 'em. It's a better deal for the middle class than the Republican plan of cutting capital gains taxes (also not paid for). Democrats should offer the deal and say so.

But if the budget rules hold and can't be broken, the other tack would be to go after the Federal Reserve. I notice that my friend Jaime Serra's successor, a Stanford economist of similar vintage, has turned the NAFTA card into $18 billion of new loans to stabilize Mexico in this moment of crisis (something I predicted, by the way, back in 1993). Why not have Greenspan or his successor do this to create jobs in, say, California, New York, New Jersey, even Texas? For that matter, why not do it for the whole American middle class, by the simple device of reversing the course of the past year and bringing interest rates back down? Congress wrote the Federal Reserve Act, and it can change it – if and as it chooses. Let the Democrats propose, say, a roll-back order on interest rates and a full sunset review of the Federal Reserve System. And let the Republicans oppose it.

The Federal Reserve Act of 1913 had one great success. It removed the subjects of interest rates and banking from politics for over eight decades. But if we can't have a real fiscal politics any more, a politics of working-class tax cuts and jobs programs and universal health care, then by all means let's go back to the 1890s, and have a politics of money and interest rates once again.

Anyone care for a crown of thorns?

(*The Texas Observer*, 13 January 1995)

Greenspan's Error

The Fed's reduction of one set of interest rates on Friday marked the beginning of the end of Alan Greenspan's war on inflation. The war began in February 1994 with the Fed's quarter point increase in the rates that banks charge one another for overnight loans and led to a doubling of those rates, to 6 percent from 3 percent. The financial markets expect further cuts.

The war was phony. So was the enemy. Despite nonstop fretting by Mr Greenspan, the Fed's chairman, no serious evidence of accelerating inflation ever emerged. For the first five months of 1995, consumer prices rose at a very modest 3.6 percent annual rate.

Inflation was never a risk. Now recession is.

The economy is more fragile than the Fed had been willing to admit. For 18 months, we have been reassured that stable growth lay ahead. But now major indicators of growth like industrial production and the sales of cars and appliances – all battered by needlessly high interest rates – are down.

Yes, the economy may rebound from its multiple slowdowns. Sales of new homes – not a generally reliable indicator – looked good in May, but most other signs are bad. On balance, the risk of recession is rising. The Fed's action showed that even its chairman had lost confidence in his earlier optimism.

The war against inflation was fought against an enemy that existed only in the imaginations and perhaps in the economic models of Mr Greenspan and his colleagues. Yet there were casualties, as in all wars.

The middle class was hit hardest by rising adjustable-rate mortgages and the falling values of stock portfolios and pension funds most of last year, because when interest rates soar stock prices tend to fall.

The five-year Federal deficit rose by some $200 billion in prospective interest costs, reversing much of the 1993 reduction. President Clinton's credibility has been damaged, for he had promised falling deficits and lower interest rates.

The Fed should have done nothing last year. Stable and low short-term rates would have generated stronger growth, lower long-term rates, higher investment and lower deficits – without bringing on inflation.

If the Fed's campaign was based on a potpourri of prejudices, hunches and assumptions, an excessive fear of rising inflation and an insufficient fear of rising unemployment, then the operating methods and the biases of the decision-makers must be questioned.

The Fed's analytic methods are dubious. It has underrated fundamental changes in the economy, and it still places too much weight on the hoary assumption that inflation will rise if unemployment falls below 6 percent. (It is currently 5.6 percent.)

The Fed's economists apparently failed to predict that wages would stand still. Since wages are always the largest element of costs, stagnating wages mean fairly stable, not inflating, prices.

There has been no increase in average wages despite falling unemployment, which reflects an increased demand for labor. Why this stagnation? One big reason is the decline of unions. Another is intense competition from imports from low-wage countries.

When Mr Greenspan next appears before Congress, he should be pressed for a full accounting of the forecasts and the theories underlying the needless war.

Congress should request the full records of Fed meetings and supporting analyses so that it and outside experts can try to understand what went wrong. And when President Clinton nominates his next candidate for the Fed's board, he and Congress should insist on a new spirit of openness in Fed deliberations.

(*New York Times*, 11 July 1995)

The Free Ride of Mr Greenspan

President Clinton is coming up on the most important appointment of his second Presidential term. Sometime soon, the term of the Chairman of the Board of Governors of the Federal Reserve System will expire. And the President must choose, whether to reappoint Alan Greenspan for four more years, or else to name a replacement. Most observers assume that Greenspan will get it, and a strange public quiet has settled over this issue.

Yet, Greenspan's track record is poor. He did act back in 1987 to prevent that October's stock market crash from turning into a depression. But he did not cut interest rates in time to prevent the recession of 1990, nor to foster recovery in 1991. And in 1994 he virtually wrecked Clinton's first term, by raising interest rates immediately after the 1993 deficit reductions, which were supposed to bring rates down, passed into law.

The destructiveness of that 1994 action is now clear. The economy is slowing on all fronts. And the Federal Reserve is again cutting interest rates, bit by bit. Whatever happened to the threat of inflation? It never existed. The economy last year was actually much more fragile than Greenspan thought. And now, because interest rates were doubled then in a false cause, stagnation and rising unemployment or even a recession this year cannot be ruled out.

Can't anyone make a mistake? Yes, but this is not the first time. A bias toward high interest rates and high unemployment is part of Mr Greenspan's personal, political, and ideological fabric. It is not accidental. It is systematic.

Personally, Alan Greenspan is a very, very conservative man, not a run-of-the-mill conservative but a philosophical extremist. Long sympathetic to the gold lobby, he once gave one thousand dollars, I'm reliably told – a thousand dollars! – to the 1984 re-election campaign of the Senate's most powerful reactionary (and closet gold bug), Senator Jesse Helms.

Indeed, Greenspan's entire professional life has been devoted to the service of the rich. His early ideology, as a follower of Ayn Rand, celebrated such service. And his later career, private and public, confirms that the rich and powerful are the people he respects, admires, and works for.

In the mid-1980s, these leanings took Greenspan into the orbit of Charles Keating, the highest flyer in the Savings and Loan industry at that time. Keating's Lincoln Savings and Loan Association was in trouble, as regulators wised up to its real estate scams. Keating needed lots of help. Greenspan, then a private consultant, obliged. On one day for which we have records, December 17, 1984, Mr Greenspan traveled to Washington to lobby on behalf of Mr Keating. Greenspan's personal fee for that one day was $12,000.

What kind of work did Keating get? On February 13, 1985, Greenspan wrote a long letter to the principal supervisory agent of the Federal Home Loan Bank in San Francisco. In it, he committed his vast prestige to the proposition that Lincoln and Keating presented 'no foreseeable risk to the Federal Savings and Loan Insurance Corporation'. The letter is a classic of Randian farrago:

1. Lincoln's new management, and that of its parent, American Continental Corporation, is seasoned and expert ...

2. The new management has a long and continuous track record of outstanding success in making sound and profitable direct investments.

3. The new management succeeded in a relatively short period of time in reviving an association that [was near] the point of insolvency.

4. The new management effectively restored the association to a vibrant and healthy state, with a strong net worth position, largely through the expert selection of sound and profitable direct investments ...

And so on.

In fact, Lincoln Savings and Loan Association was at the heart of a massive fraud; those 'sound and profitable direct investments' were mostly worthless. The collapse, when it came, by itself cost American taxpayers over three billion dollars, more than any other single S&L. It resulted in more than six felony convictions, including that of Charles Keating.

Greenspan's reconfirmation would come before the Senate Banking Committee, whose chairman, Senator Alfonse D'Amato, is the chief inquisitor into that fringe of the S&L scandal known as Whitewater. Lincoln's failure was roughly a hundred times more costly. And Greenspan is being considered – amazingly enough by a Democratic President – for reappointment to the single greatest position of financial trust in the entire world.

It would be nice to think that, if the occasion arises, the Senate Banking Committee will investigate carefully what Mr Greenspan really knew of Lincoln Savings and Loan and about Mr Charles Keating back in February of 1985. The Senators should ask what Greenspan did to assure himself of the accuracy of his knowledge, before drafting his influential letter and before collecting another Keating fee.

Weak ethics or poor judgment? Hard to say. Charitably, I'd guess that Mr Greenspan was simply seduced by Mr Keating. But however that may be, so long as those old S&L coals continue to smolder, Greenspan's Keating connection is another good reason why Clinton should pick somebody else to chair the Federal Reserve.

Indeed, given what we know so far, the republic would be safer if the President named his wife to the job.

(*The Texas Observer*, 23 February 1996)

There's Some Good News That's Bad News

Now why (I hear you ask) is good news for the economy bad news for the markets? Why, in particular, did the stock market drop a hundred points on March 9, the very day that unemployment was reported to have fallen to its lowest level in years?

One possibility is that the stock-owning public is composed mainly of Bad People, who can't stand Christmas or anything that smacks of good fortune for others, and who throw tantrums when such events occur. We might call this the Grinch theory.

A slightly more rational thought would take note of the social position of the stock-owners. It is a fact, of course, that in a capitalist economy stock is capital, and its owners are the capitalists. Capitalists hire labor, and needless to say they prefer not to have to pay too much. A strong jobs report might put them in fear of that next union vote, that next strike, that next negotiation. Higher wages mean lower profits, and lower profits mean lower valuations on the stock market.

Then there is the Newton's law hypothesis: what goes up must come down. By this argument, the good news really is good news, and that's the problem. Stock-owners, you see, have already made a forecast of the future, over, say, a year or two ahead. One day's news doesn't change the forecast. But it does change the *balance* between what has already happened, within the forecast, and what remains to happen. So the unexpected element of good news in the forecast is subtracted from the expected future, or, if you like, it is transfered from the future to the past. That being so, the future that remains, under the forecast, now looks worse than it did before. And the stock market must decline to reflect this.

I don't actually believe any of these stories. The first is silly. The second presupposes the resurgent power of workers to be greater than it really is. And the third gives people credit for greater consistency and calculating power than they really have.

What then? There is a simpler and more persuasive story behind this phenomenon, and his name is Alan Greenspan.

One of the stablest and most predictable relationships in all of economics is that between the price of bonds and the interest rate. Raise the interest rate, and the price of a bond must fall. Lower the interest rate, and the price of bonds must rise. This is a well-known and a very elementary fact.

But many stocks, especially the blue-chips that make up the Dow Jones Index, also behave quite like long-term bonds. Barring a real disaster, they pay a steady dividend, year in and year out, despite fluctuations in the earnings of the company that issued them. And they are held by many people for income, for precisely this reason. That annual dividend looks just like an interest payment, only it's higher.

But that being so a prospective change in the interest rate will affect the price of these stocks much as it affects the price of long-term bonds. And that's where Alan Greenspan comes in.

Greenspan, of course, *is* a Grinch. He doesn't like Christmas. He is pathologically averse to full employment, pathologically over-anxious about inflation. His policies are the reason, for the most part, that unemployment has stayed high and that wages have not risen in the past decade. And he is determined to keep things that way. Moreover, everyone knows it: Greenspan's sour reaction to good economic news is well-documented and extremely predictable.

Therefore, it is not necessary for stock-owners to be Grinches themselves, or to fear rising wages and prices, or to calculate every element of a complex forecast. It is only necessary for them to know that Alan Greenspan is and does these things.

Given good news, Greenspan will very predictably wish to raise interest rates. Under a sufficient influx of bad news, he may eventually decide to lower them. But either way the decision for stockholders is clear. If the news is good, that means a rise in the rate of interest may be on the way. And that, by itself, will cause the stock market to fall.

Lucky the effect doesn't last; the market bounced back on Monday. But that's another story. It may be that, on a weekend's reflection, the markets realized that the Federal Reserve Board will soon have two new faces on it, Alice Rivlin and Lawrence Meyer. Possibly, they may combine with incumbent governors Lawrence Lindsey and Janet Yellen to form a pro-growth, pro-job, lower-interest-rate majority on the Board. If that happens, well, happy days are here again.

(*Newsday*, 27 March 1996)

Greenspan's Whim

Why did Alan Greenspan raise interest rates? Because he could. Because two of the more independent members of his Board, the pro-growth conservative Lawrence Lindsey and the moderate Janet Yellen, have departed. Because he has been under pressure from banks and bond traders for two years; why not throw them a bone? Because he knows the Clinton Administration will say and do nothing in protest. And, especially, because he can get away with it.

Here is the Federal Reserve's official statement on March 24: 'The action was taken in light of persisting strength in demand, which is progressively increasing the risk of inflationary imbalances developing in the economy ...' These words had been carefully foreshadowed in Greenspan's Congressional testimony four days previously, which is why the action was not a surprise.

But elsewhere in that statement, Greenspan had offered no serious evidence of rising inflation. Instead, he spoke of the low and 'benign' inflation of the past year, and the fact that 'the rate of pay increase [in 1996] was still markedly less than historical relationships ... would have predicted'. Looking forward, Greenspan stated that 'competitive pressures here and abroad should continue to act as a restraint on inflation in the months ahead' – citing particularly improved supplies of oil and food.

The only risks Greenspan sees are these. First, 'a continued tight labor market', second, the 'scheduled increase in the minimum wage later this year'. And third, the possibility that 'larger increases in fringe benefits could put upward pressure on overall compensation'.

The gentleman could not have been more clear. He is not concerned about inflation – there is no serious risk of that. He is concerned about the possibility, remote and uncertain though it is, that the American worker might start to demand, and receive, a slightly increased *share* of the economic growth that has occurred over the past seven years. Repressing wages is the essential thing, and the way to do that is to slow economic growth, raise unemployment, and make sure that the job insecurity which Greenspan explicitly credits for suppressing wage growth – his words – does not diminish or disappear.

Repressing wages is not, however, the only thing. Greenspan is also the tax collector for the commercial banks, who instantly raised their prime rate and thus their revenue from every adjustable-rate loan they make. (Deposit rates will be very slow to follow). Greenspan has also stated, in so many words, that he wants to scare middle-class American families out of the stock market. Why? They are doing too well there. Back to the banks with you – and to their measly money market funds! Finally, the market churning that accompanies speculation over the Fed's next rate move is good for bond traders, who pined and whined all the way through the quiet times of the past two years.

'*L'Etat, c'est moi*', could well have been uttered by Alan Greenspan this week.

(*New York Times*, 27 March 1997)

Greenspan's Glasnost

There they were, the high priests of the American Economics Association, a score of old men lined up at the head table like the Politburo atop Lenin's tomb, with the same bad haircuts, black horn-rims and blank expressions. Speaking before this geriatric welcoming committee last week, Alan Greenspan managed to imitate the early Mikhail Gorbachev with surprising flair. I listened and was amazed.

We were in Chicago, where economists teach that the markets are rational, efficient and benign. We were in Chicago, where financial crises are said to have no real effects. We were in Chicago, where doctrine holds that monetary policy cannot even affect employment or output except in the very short run, and that the right Federal Reserve policy is one that pursues stable prices to the exclusion of every other economic objective.

Against this nonsense, Greenspan made arguments that came straight from John Maynard Keynes, Hyman Minsky and John Kenneth Galbraith. Following Keynes, he spoke of the dangers when speculators flee real investments to the illusory safety of money, and of the risks when falling product prices bring rising 'real' interest rates that cannot be offset by easy money policies because the nominal interest rate cannot fall below zero. Following Minsky, who died in 1996, he spoke of the dangers of 'debt deflation'. And following Galbraith *père*, to my personal delight, he noted that the Great Depression of the 1930s originated in the Great Crash of 1929, a fact obvious to ordinary students of history but which several luminaries of that head table had been at pains in years past to deny.

Greenspan's speech thus acknowledged that the Asian crisis threatens our system, and not merely because the slumping Pacific Rim means fewer US exports. More serious dangers come from the repercussions through the capital markets and on the price level. With falling stock and other asset prices, mounting debt troubles for American investors will soon appear. With falling product prices – a phenomenon underlined a few days later by the news that wholesale prices fell in the United States for 1997 as a whole – real interest rates are already rising. No one can say whether, or when, the financial disturbances on the other side of the Pacific may trigger a major crisis here. But the risk exists; in history the belief that capitalism has triumphed for all time characteristically precedes disaster.

Equally important was what Greenspan did not say. He spoke not at all about 'irrational exuberance', inflation risks, or of the natural rate of unemployment, a doctrine formally declared dead the next day at a memorial lunch in honor of 1996 Nobel prizewinner William Vickrey. And Greenspan issued a vigorous if subtle repudiation of those who would substitute for the judgment of the Bureau of Labor Statistics in the measurement of price indices (specifically, the Boskin commission, at least two of whose members were at that head table) or insist on an exclusive inflation rate target for the Federal Reserve. There was too much uncertainty, he said, in the measurement of price changes to make them into the sole focus of central bank policy.

In short, it seemed that for once the top leader of the Federal Reserve was looking forward alertly to the grave dangers we now face. In this, Greenspan stands in contrast to President Clinton, who issued a balanced budget last week to the usual idiotic fanfares; to the IMF, whose self-contradictory analysis and prescriptions for deflation in Korea can be read on the Internet (www.chosun.com); and to those in Congress, like Senator Lauch Faircloth, who imagine that allowing free markets to deflate the world economy would be a good thing; and to those, like Senator Connie Mack, who would rewrite the Fed's charter to make it focus exclusively on prices. Greenspan also stands opposed to those within the Federal Reserve, a clique of regional bank presidents for the most part, who argue reflexively for higher interest rates, meeting after meeting, irrespective of changing conditions in the world outside.

The clear implication, though Greenspan did not spell it out, is that the world may shortly need an expansionary policy – dare I say a global Keynesianism? – led by the United States. Lower interest rates should come soon, to offset the rising real rate as prices fall, to relieve debt burdens denominated in dollars and to try to stabilize the capital markets. But fiscal policy, now stuck on the idea that the US Federal Government should be the only economic entity in the history of capitalism that doesn't routinely issue new debt, may also have to expand, to help offset our lost export sales with some combination of new public investment and even, yes, perhaps a tax reduction (for instance, raising the Earned Income Tax Credit).

Will we get these things, and enough of them, and before it's too late? The omens are not good. Keynes, Minsky and Galbraith are out of fashion. We live in a time of triumphalism about free markets, combined with balanced-budget fetishism and hard-money ascendancy in policy discussion. Our elected leaders, the Republicans in Congress and the Democrat in the White House, share this complacent consensus. The IMF, out on the front line, insists on policies that will not restore market confidence in Asia but that can only depress the Pacific Rim countries and make the crisis there even worse. The economics profession, epitomized by that moribund head table, has been for the most part uselessly silent so far.

Whether the Federal Reserve will rise to this occasion remains to be seen. Still, it is some comfort that, at the peak of his reputation, power and influence, Alan Greenspan is asking the right questions at last.

(*The Texas Observer*, 30 January 1998)

The Butterfly Effect

James K. Galbraith and George Purcell

Small actions can have large consequences. The mathematics of chaos teaches that a butterfly, flapping its wings in Brazil, can set off a chain of events leading to a hurricane at Cape Fear. They call this the 'butterfly effect'.

On March 24, 1997, the butterfly was named Alan Greenspan. That day, he flapped his wings just once, raising the interest rate by one-quarter of one percentage point, about 5 percent of then-prevailing values.

Global currency instability started just about then. Figure 4 shows the daily movement of exchange rates for seven currencies: the Australian and Taiwan dollars, and the national currencies of the Philippines, Malaysia, Thailand, Korea and Indonesia. The Thai crisis hit three months later amidst speculation that the Fed might act again. After that, the yen, the Australian and Taiwan dollars, and the national currencies of the Philippines, Malaysia, Thailand, Korea and Indonesia all declined, leaving only the pound and the dollar flying high.

Thus the so-called 'Asian crisis' was not restricted to Asia. Nor did the markets suddenly discover that particular countries suffered from inefficiency, corruption, deficits, inflation, or other internal disorders. Instead, Asian and non-Asian currencies have moved in striking parallel, often day by day. The differences were of degree: since March the currencies of Europe, Japan, Australia and Taiwan have fallen about 20 percent; a cluster of the Philippines, Malaysia, Korea and Thailand fell 40 percent, and Indonesia fell 80 percent.

In short, currencies collapsed in proportion to their dependence on American capital. Those hit hardest were those that have relied most on our investments, that had the least resident wealth of their own, that were most caught up in construction booms financed by

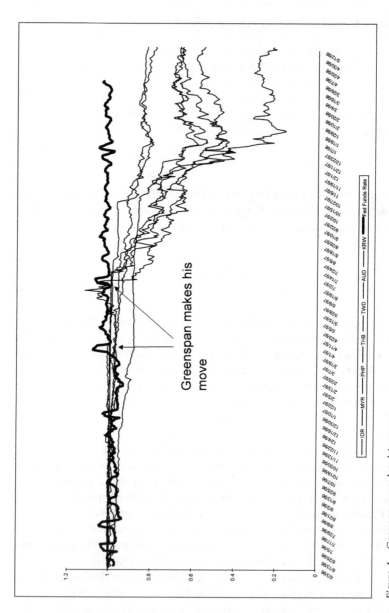

Figure 4 Greenspan makes his move

short-term inflows. When US interest rates started to rise, dollar-sensitive investors came home. The dollar went up, and its closest dependencies, like Suharto's rupiah, were the greatest victims. This is a crisis of the American empire.

It is also a crisis of the 'Washington consensus', that doctrine of deregulation and open capital markets. Much nonsense has been written about the collapse of the Asian development model – a collapse which, for unexplained reasons, has not taken down Taiwan, or China. Reforms in Seoul and Djakarta may be necessary, but they alone cannot cure a problem caused primarily by policies in the large financial centers.

Since the Fed's action triggered vast capital inflows into the United States, it assuredly helped to fuel the stock market boom. But the rise in demand for dollars hurt our productive economy, and the effects are now surfacing in a vast increase in the US trade deficit, as exports tumble and cheapened imports flood our markets. These consequences will multiply if we fail to act quickly – and correctly.

Today, some say US interest rates should rise. Rate increase enthusiasts claim that this would deflate our stock bubble. But the short-run effect could be the opposite; a higher interest rate could drain more capital from overseas and push stocks upward. And that effect would come at the cost of yet more collapse in the world economy and a larger trade deficit for the United States.

In the end, down this path lies disaster. If the first dose fails and rate increases are repeated, eventually the structure of US household debts, already at dangerous levels, is bound to crack. The collapse that would follow would be long lasting. It could mean the end of the dollar era, the end of the postwar growth age, and the end of the global markets for aircraft, computers, communications systems and other products that give us our technological edge in the world economy today.

Alan Greenspan seems aware of these dangers: he spoke of them vividly in an important speech six months ago. But there remains an intransigent faction at the Federal Reserve that favors higher interest rates under all conditions. And so the debate is between those who say 'raise rates' and those who say, 'not yet'. Under these conditions, to hold the line is the best Greenspan can do, and such a stalemate must always end in a rate increase – never, until much too late, in a rate cut.

There are, so far as we can tell, no voices at the Fed calling for the rate cuts that, we believe, global stability and domestic prosperity demand. And this is not the only necessary step not yet on anyone's agenda. A Tobin tax on capital flows and speculative transactions, long recommended by many economists, could help steady the global markets – but we are more likely to get destabilizing tax cuts on capital gains. Special steps toward Russia are urgently needed, as that giant country, a security issue for the entire globe, continues its slide toward disaster. The Treasury's recent intervention to bolster the Japanese yen was one good step, but more may be needed.

By stemming capital inflows and stabilizing our trading partners, the actions we recommend might send US stock prices downward at first – a boom based mainly on capital inflows will not continue when they stop. But over a longer time frame, stock prices will recover if our economic growth is sustained by an early recovery of the world economy, of other currencies and of our export markets. The alternative: more global instability and more of our own debt-driven bubble, followed by a prolonged collapse, could be chaos.

(*The Texas Observer*, 3 July 1998)

The Credit, Where Credit is Due

Phil Gramm said it precisely, 'If you were forced to narrow down the credit for the golden age that we find ourselves living in, I think there are many people who would be due credit, and many more who would claim credit.'

Gramm went on to praise Alan Greenspan, as one might expect at the man's fourth confirmation hearing. But *credit* – the willingness and ability of the American household to incur debt – is the thing. It is *credit* that accounts for the record-high homeownership we now enjoy, for our new cars and appliances, and (in part) for our bloated stock prices. In comparison with credit, Mr Greenspan is a bit player.

And the fact that American capitalism runs on credit is also its vulnerable point. So long as house prices and stock prices are rising, household balance sheets look great. But when they stop rising, while debt continues to build, then credit becomes a burden. And if those prices fall, the great American debt machine could be in trouble.

Which raises a question. Why are Mr Greenspan and his colleagues hell-bent on higher interest rates? Higher interest rates will squeeze middle-income families out of the housing market. They make every sort of durable goods purchase more expensive. And they don't just depress the stock market, they skew the distribution of stock prices. Just look at the opposed movement of the NASDAQ (up) and the blue chips (down) in the past six months. A higher interest rate means a higher *required* rate of return, and that causes speculators to concentrate their activities. Rising interest rates don't pop a bubble, they feed it. At least for a time.

Greenspan was asked by Senator Charles Schumer whether he was concerned about margin lending, which jumped sharply in the final months of last year (in conformity with the theory just stated, this occurred as interest rates were being pushed up). Yes, it turns out, the Chairman is concerned. But since raising margin requirements is not a 'perfect' solution, the issue remains under study. But in the meantime higher interest rates – a far less perfect solution – will soon be decided once again.

The 1978 Humphrey-Hawkins Full Employment and Balanced Growth Act stipulates three main goals for economic policy: 'full employment', 'balanced growth', and 'reasonable price stability'. Remarkably, we have two out of three: full employment and reasonable price stability, a magic combination that so many economists deemed impossible for so long. But balanced growth eludes us. And unbalanced growth, relying so heavily on household debt, cannot endure.

Mr Greenspan testified, and the press faithfully reported, that the purpose of his present policies is to prolong the expansion. But the effect of raising interest rates is to curtail, not to prolong, our expansion. It is, as other press reports plainly state, to slow economic growth and bring the expansion to an end. And when rising interest rates finally achieve this, what then?

Like all golden ages, the one Senator Gramm described so aptly will end. We are not on a sustainable track. And when the Fed majority that favors slower growth and higher unemployment finally gets its way, they will produce not a slowdown but a slump, not a plateau in stock prices but a crash. That could be a year or more away. But when it comes, Mr Greenspan will surely regret that he didn't ride off into the sunset this year, his reputation as the greatest Fed chief ever serenely intact.

(The Street.com, 27 January 2000)

Stop the Sabotage Coming from the Fed

The scene for November is nearly set. South Carolina did for George W. Bush what it did for Bob Dole: it sent him onwards, born again at Bob Jones University and wrapped in the Confederate flag. But the New Hampshire verdict, repeated at Michigan, will remain the authentic one. Like Dole, Bush is a weak candidate who will have to be rescued again and again from a popular insurgent by party leaders and the God squad.

On the Democratic side, Vice President Gore has campaigned effectively since New Hampshire, helped by a press that lost interest in my man Bradley. Gore has emerged as a strong candidate, like him or not. He secured his base early, held on to it, and can now move toward the independent vote, rather than away from it as Bush has been obliged to do.

So supposing it will be Gore and Bush in November, what will the issue be? In the immortal Carvillism, 'The Economy, Stupid'. Gore will run on the long boom, full employment without inflation, the high stock market, e-commerce and e-wealth. It will be no contest. If the boom holds.

But what if it doesn't?

A sword hangs over Al Gore. It is the interest rate, the instrument of a relentless Federal Reserve campaign against full employment. Since productivity growth is high and inflation is nil, the Fed can barely pretend that it has real reasons for jacking interest rates to the sky. There is no crisis, not even a problem. The Fed has merely decided to end the long boom.

The first victim is the stock market. Rising interest rates have been killing off the blue-chips for months, while actually pumping up the tech sector as speculators doubled their bets. But a bubble squeezed in this way pops all the sooner. The end may be underway now. Crashing stock prices will deflate the 'wealth effect' – cutting hard not only at speculators but also at the pensions of the newly retired and the pension funds of millions who hope to retire some day.

Next, high interest rates will hit small business, housing mortgages and car loans. They will squeeze middle-income families with small portfolios and big debts. Only a few will actually have lost their jobs by November – but that doesn't matter. With the crunch on and anxieties high, Al Gore will lose the number one pillar of his campaign.

Is the Fed doing this on purpose? Motives cannot be proven. But what matters are effects, not causes. The Fed's actions will not preserve – they will destroy – full employment without inflation. They will also eventually destroy the budget surplus, and the small wage gains and progress made since 1994 in reducing inequalities of pay. They could undo, and in a fairly short time, the entire reputation of the Administration of Bill Clinton and Al Gore.

I do not blame Alan Greenspan personally. Like him or not, the long boom is his baby; full employment without inflation is his accomplishment. Since Greenspan's own reputation will be destroyed, along with Clinton's, if the economy goes sour, he may well have mixed emotions about what the Fed is doing now.

But Greenspan is only the Chair of the Fed's Open Market Committee. And that peculiar decision-making body is heavily influenced by the twelve presidents of the regional Fed banks, men who are not appointed by Clinton and not accountable to anyone beyond their local, banker-dominated boards. Two of these curious policymakers are veterans of Reagan's Council of Economic Advisers; many others are simple-minded reactionaries who seem to get most of their financial ideas from the country club set. On the Board of Governors, Clinton's three surviving Democrats are political lightweights. Greenspan must therefore manage an FOMC with an aggressive right-wing majority; he could hardly act otherwise even if he disagreed with them.

Can anything be done? Yes. The key to this situation – to the fate of the long boom, to the reputation of his Presidency and also to the election – remains in President Clinton's hands. There are two gaping vacancies on the Board of Governors of the Federal Reserve System. Clinton could fill them now – if necessary by recess appointment since one nomination is already sitting under Phil Gramm who shows no sign of moving on it – with independent, pro-growth economists like Jane D'Arista of the Financial Markets Center or Thomas Palley of the AFL-CIO.

A couple of good new people could galvanize the Federal Reserve Board. They could keep the saboteurs in check – and save the country into the bargain.

(*The Texas Observer*, 17 March 2000)

The Charge of the Fed Brigade

Where, oh where, is Alfred Lord Tennyson when we need him now?

> NASDAQ to the right of them
> OPEC to the left of them.
> Volleyed and thundered …

And so the Open Market Charge goes forward. Just as the oil price eases up, ensuring benign inflation numbers ahead, just as the tech stocks tumble, taking a little edge off the bubble, the Fed raises interest rates again.

> Forward the Fed Brigade!
> Was there a man dismay'd

All my adult life economists have preached that America's great problem was a slow rate of productivity growth. Wage growth above productivity! That was the eternal danger, the mortal risk, the root cause of dread inflation.

Where are those economists now? Suddenly, productivity growth is up – and Alan Greenspan now tells us that a high productivity growth rate is our problem. Why? Because, he says, it adds too much to household income. Or, as the Reuters story has it, too much to 'expectations of future corporate earnings, thus inflating stock prices and financing the unprecedented boom in consumer spending'.

> Not tho' the people knew,
> Someone had blunder'd

137

Productivity growth is about aggregate *supply*. It has nothing to do with income! It has nothing to do with stock prices or corporate earnings! When productivity increases, and runs ahead of wages, prices must *fall*. Or wages can go up too, if they will, *without* putting pressure on prices. Increased productivity is a free gift. It is anti-inflation insurance. It validates the policies that produced the higher rate of output. Or so I thought.

Put another way, how can low productivity growth *and* high productivity growth *both* be causes of inflation? (Particularly when, as any observer can plainly see, there is no inflation?)

> Theirs not to make reply
> Theirs not to reason why

And will they do it again, six weeks from now? You bet they will.

> Half a point, half a point,
> Half a point onward.

(James K. Galbraith is not particularly fond of Tennyson. The Street.com, 21 March 2000)

We Cannot Have Discipline So We Must Have Pain

I have at least two friends – divorced women in their fifties, intellectuals, with literary and cultural interests – who put their nest eggs into NASDAQ stocks earlier this year. *Ouch!* Neither of them was rich, nor ever destined to be. Now they will be somewhat less so.

In the long history of manias and speculations, the info-tech boom was far from being the worst to come along. Past frenzies have centered on real estate in swamps and suburbs (Florida, Texas), on ephemera (tulips), or on the pursuit of the world's most useless metal (gold). In most cases, fraud was a dominant motive force.

In the tech boom, the beneficiaries were mainly small companies staffed by nerds and b-school grads. Most of them were trying to make a product; and some of them succeeded. Fraud there was, but most of it was of the genial, optimistic, borderline sort that characterizes every long shot – who knows if this stuff will work? Not a bad way, all in all, for bright and ambitious young people to spend their time. They weren't building nukes, after all, or dealing drugs, or running numbers.

And could they have succeeded? In many cases, they might have, given time, money and reasonable expectations. Stock offerings raised cash, which was then used to fund operations. The NASDAQ was a machine that converted naive hopes and blind optimism into payrolls, the payrolls were placed as bets on gadgets and lines of code. Not all of those bets were honest, and not all of the honest ones were any good. But some of them were.

Alas, tech companies can only absorb so much cash at a time. Beyond a certain point, there was much more money available than could be used. The time to payoff grows longer, necessarily, as the bets grow more exotic. Good management of the tech boom would have required measuring out the financial injections, stretching them through time, and keeping a lid on unrealistic expectations of gain.

This was Mr Alan Greenspan's responsibility. And he blew it.

For the financial markets, it's give an inch, take a mile. If 20 percent gain is possible, why not 40 percent? Margin lending is a device for doubling your bets. But only for a limited time; if the inflows do not continually accelerate, a reckoning must come. Everyone buying on margin knows this; they all calculate that they can get out before the crash. In the meantime, more and more of the money flows to projects less and less likely to succeed before the bills come due.

This is why Henry Reuss – the former Chair of the House Banking and Joint Economic Committees of Congress – and I were calling last autumn for a sharp rise in the margin requirement. We saw the danger, and we said so. The Federal Reserve ignored us. They made excuses, citing 'academic studies' on the ineffectiveness of the margin rules. No such studies on raising interest rates were ever commissioned. Interest rates went up, margin requirements did not: a formula for disaster. Margin loans exploded.

The Federal Reserve knew this. It did nothing. As an institution, it deliberately and willfully took the speculators' part.

And now, the crash has come – sooner than I expected, but for reasons both predictable and predicted. It was all perfectly needless, and perfectly avoidable, even up to the past few weeks. Mr Greenspan's motto is: We Cannot Have Discipline So We Must Have Pain.

I don't think – I could be wrong – that the rest of the economy will go down. At least not right away. But the tech sector, an innocent and largely cheerful creation of a hopeful moment in our economic history, is deeply wounded. It is a casualty of the feckless Fed, a blot on Greenspan's reputation, and a sign that when the chips are down, the brokers and the bankers win out over the nerds and the b-school graduates every time.

Not to mention the financial innocents who piled into the NASDAQ at the top.

(*The Texas Observer*, 8 April 2000)

The Swiss Guard

Have you noticed all the establishment liberals defending the Fed? They have enlisted as Greenspan's Swiss Guard, brass helmets shining, pikes at the ready. To bash those who would bash the Fed – this has become their holy task.

Just last week, George L. Perry of Brookings was quoted, in distinctly theocratic terms:

> *There is a tendency* to go too far and talk as if we're in a world where there are no limits and where we don't need to think in terms of the old concepts at all ...

Then on the Op-Ed page of the *New York Times*, I found Alice Rivlin:

> *Other critics regard* all interest rate increases as pernicious and dismiss the risks to future expansion from incipient inflation, extreme worker scarcity and consumer spending out of paper wealth.

In my local paper, the *New Republic*'s columnist Matthew Miller – he used to work for Rivlin – was even harsher:

> The surest test of the Fed-bashers' confusion (did someone say 'intellectual corruption'?) is simple: They've never met an interest rate hike they can support.

As to solutions, Perry knows infallibly what must be done: 'we have to tighten monetary policy to slow the economy'. Rivlin calls it a 'no-brainer': 'The economy is growing too fast, and the Federal Reserve needs to keep raising the short-term interest rate – the only instrument it has – until the economy slows to a more sustainable pace.' Miller says the economy is growing 'far beyond anyone's guess' of potential, and raising rates is therefore 'only prudent'.

Convincing this may sound (did someone say 'shrill'?) but recent history provides no support for the slow-it-down prescription. Rivlin concedes this: 'economists used to say that unemployment rates below 5 percent, or growth rates above 3 percent, would cause inflation, but those limits have been breached for some time without ill effect ...' Miller, too, confesses: 'Nobody knows just how low joblessness can go in this new era without igniting inflation.' (*Ergo: inflation has not ignited yet.*) It is, to choose words precisely, a matter of faith.

So let's take up the various arguments on their merits. Shall we? Here are 9.5 theses for the Brookings door.

1. *Is the economy growing too fast?* 7.3 percent in the fourth quarter sounds high. But we already have the first quarter numbers: growth slowed to 5.4 percent. In 1984, 7 percent growth rate continued all year, then slowed on its own. In the late 1960s, unemployment was below 4 percent for 3 years. There was a bit of inflation then – but there was also a war on.

2. *Is there incipient inflation today?* Rivlin says so, but that was based on the March CPI. Producer prices declined in April – a fact already known when she published, but she didn't mention it. And then consumer price inflation practically disappeared in April too, just before the Fed hiked rates.

3. *Why did inflation disappear?* Oil prices went down. And productivity growth has been high enough to prevent high actual growth rates from pushing up other costs. When productivity growth keeps up with output growth, there will be, by definition, no inflation problem.

4. *Do we have extreme worker scarcity?* If so, why aren't wages rising faster than prices? Unit labor costs rose only 1.8 percent in the first quarter; in the previous two quarters they declined.

5. *Should we be concerned about the wealth effect?* To quote from Dubya Bush, 'Maybe, maybe not.' But if so, short-term interest rates are *not* the only instrument the Fed has. To cool the tech stocks late last year, it could have raised margin requirements. (Forgive me, dear readers, I have said this before.)

6. *Will rate hikes actually slow the economy to a sustainable pace?* Sad to say, this has never happened. In the short run, knowing that interest rates will rise, borrowers rush to beat the increases;

spending and growth continue to go up, not down. (Same story as in 1994, incidentally.) Eventually there follows a market break, investment slump, and recession. (In 1995 we got lucky: the Fed stopped raising rates before the bad effects took hold.)

7. *What would happen next, if the Fed didn't raise rates?* I don't know. Why not wait to find out? My guess is that the economy would slow somewhat on its own, both output and productivity growth, without accelerating inflation. The slumping stock market and budget surpluses are already dragging down the growth rate, a point Rivlin also concedes. In other words, we will get where Rivlin wants, even if nothing is done.

8. *Is it intellectually corrupt to oppose higher rates?* Personally I have consistently opposed higher interest rates. I did ask Matt Miller, as a cross-check on his simple test, whether he had ever *criticized* Fed policy; the candid answer was no. Neither, I'm fairly sure, have Alice or George. But in all cases, though, that's consistency, not corruption.

9. *And come to think of it, who are all these supposed Fed critics?* I feel pretty lonely out here most days. Where is Al Gore? Where are the Democrats in Congress? And where is the *AFL-CIO*? Why are my left-liberal friends wasting themselves on China? While my establishment-liberal friends go heretic-hunting for Greenspan? Why am I forced into a god-help-me alliance with the unrepentant Reaganite supply-sider *Larry Kudlow*?

9.5. *Well, I'll take Kudlow if I have to.* Larry and I know, at least, what higher interest rates will do, unless this campaign stops soon. We both lived through it in the Reagan years. The long-run effect of a continuing campaign to raise rates is not sustainable growth but recession, with rising unemployment, mass bankruptcies, and a return to big deficits. This happened in 1970, in 1974, in 1980, in 1981–82 and in 1990.

The hard fact is, these folks crash land just about every single time. And that is the real reason why we heretics oppose the Fed's policy. We have looked at history. And we oppose a course of action that has almost always, in the past, led to disaster.

(James K. Galbraith believes in full employment, balanced growth, reasonable price stability, low interest rates and the great Ogden Nash couplet: 'if there is one virtue to Americans unknown, it is: leave well enough, alone'. The Street.com, May 2000)

Watching Greenspan Grow

Greenspan: the Man Behind Money, by Justin Martin (Cambridge: Perseus Publishing, 2000)
Maestro: Greenspan's Fed and the American Boom, by Bob Woodward (New York: Simon and Schuster, 2000)

For those seeking a personal portrait of America's maximum economic policymaker, Justin Martin's biography will be hard to improve on. Informed and sympathetic, Martin traces the webs of Alan Greenspan's personal and professional lives: his early days in jazz and Objectivism, his roots as an economist in the Conference Board and old-style business cycle studies of Arthur Burns, his ties to five Presidents and his liaisons and enduring friendships with interesting, intelligent, attractive and loyal women.

Greenspan emerges here as observers usually find him: reserved, dispassionate, thoughtful, not very pretentious, an even-tempered professional and a stable inner self, oddly at home in the outsized trappings of Chairman of the Board of Governors of the Federal Reserve. As my mother reported after he attended the annual Galbraith Harvard commencement party in 1999: 'After all the harsh things you've written about him I was quite prepared to dislike him, but he was very nice. And his wife is nice, too.'

Another good thing about Martin's book: it is short. How much of this sort of stuff does one need to know? If there were some thread of intellectual or moral drama running through Greenspan's life, an important book or even a cache of letters, a scientific contribution, a bit of hardship or of sacrifice, a touch of scandal, of lust, betrayal, unusual venality or crime – then he would doubtless merit a longer treatment. But there appears to be nothing of this sort. Even Greenspan's connections to the darker aspects of his associates' lives – to the inbred sex of the Randians, to the Nixon of Watergate, to Charles Keating (for whom he consulted) all seem marked by the detachment for which he is more generally known. The result may be admirable, in its way, but it does not make for a gripping read.

And what is the relationship between Alan Greenspan and the American boom? Now *there* (to an economist) is a gripping topic. Bob Woodward thinks he knows: the one is the author of the other. And so, while oddly the word 'Objectivism' does not appear in his index, Woodward gives us Greenspan as an Ayn Rand hero, an all-seeing, all-knowing, all-wise figure; The Man Who Made Capitalism Work.

Shaman would be, on the whole, a better title for this book. Woodward sets the tone on the opening page:

> Not only is [Greenspan] a major figure in the world's economic past, he is central to its future. He has been frank enough to stand before the new and amazing economic circumstances that he helped to create and in the end to declare them a mystery. It is impossible to account fully for the continuing high growth, record employment, low inflation and high stock market.

Impossible to account for? It might have been useful to try a few numbers. These would have shown that while the expansion of the 1990s was quite long, it was never a time of very high rates of growth. The sixties, for instance, had a better growth record, leading to unemployment below 4 percent for three full years beginning in 1966. And low inflation is the norm, not the exception, in postwar America – apart from the nasty period from 1969 to 1980, marked by war (Vietnam), war again (Arab-Israel), and revolution (Iran). Woodward might also have asked whether it was likely that stock prices would stay up forever. The later 1990s were a good time, certainly, while they lasted. Amazing and unprecedented they were not.

But Woodward does not review any numbers. Instead, to set up the amazing character of events, he repeats the apologetics offered over the years by certain economists, concerning the inflationary dangers of low unemployment, and therefore their surprise when full employment did not, in fact, produce inflation. Woodward swallows his apologetics without salt. In 1994, for instance:

> All the economic models built on years of history showed there was a limit to how high growth could go without triggering inflation. To complicate matters, the economists believed – and recent American history showed ... there was a limit on how low the unemployment rate could go without triggering inflation, and it was thought the range was 6 to 7 percent. (p. 122)

This was, of course, completely in error as later events were to prove. But the habitual morbidity of the economists, which Alan Greenspan shared, was complicated in his particular case by a propensity to see the shadows of inflation itself in every dark statistical corner. Thus, as far back as 1987, Greenspan would read the entrails:

> The economy in August of 1987 was going too strong. There were no measurable signs of inflation yet, but the seeds were there. Greenspan was sure of it. He saw from economic data reports that the lead times on deliveries of goods from manufacturers to suppliers or stores were increasing, just starting to go straight up ... He had seen this happen too many times in past decades, so he felt he knew exactly what he was looking at. The pattern in economic history was almost invariably that you got a bang as prices headed up, resulting in 8 or 9 percent annual inflation – a disaster that would destroy the purchasing power of the dollar. The question now, for Greenspan, was how hard the Federal Reserve could lean against the economy to slow it down ... (p. 29).

When, exactly, did inflation in Alan Greenspan's professional lifetime exceed 8 percent? The answer is, twice: in 1973–74 and in 1978–81. Those two episodes were related to oil prices, and they presaged recession, not runaway boom. Did Greenspan really think this way, imagining hyperinflation on the basis of mis-remembered history and one stray indicator? It is hard to believe. To paraphrase John Maynard Keynes on Stanley Baldwin, when Mr Woodward talks about the ideas of Mr Greenspan, it not only is nonsense that he is speaking, but it *sounds like nonsense* to any ordinary uninstructed person who takes the trouble to consider the question with a fresh and open mind. The only question is, *whose nonsense*? Woodward's, or Greenspan's?

Inflation in 1987 did not reach 5 percent. But the rise in interest rates in September helped trigger the stock crash in October and a near collapse of the financial system. Woodward's day-to-day account of these events is pretty gripping. But he never suggests that Fed policy might have been different from what it was; still less that the Fed ought to have known better, than to do what it did.

For Woodward, Greenspan is essentially infallible, 'obviously the best numbers man around'. Time and again, though, the great one is bedeviled by critics. Under Reagan, there were Richard Darman and Manley Johnson. Under Bush, there were David Mullins and Nicholas Brady. Under Clinton, there were Alan Blinder and also on at least one occasion, Al Gore. All pressed for lower interest rates or against increases, for stronger growth, for less unemployment. Greenspan in each instance resisted. In 1988, 'Greenspan feared an outburst of inflation'. But there was none. In 1992, Greenspan stalled on interest rate cuts for months; recovery did not come. In 1994, 'high inflation could not be detected, but he suspected it was around the corner'. It was not.

History, in each case, shows that the critics were right. On a close reading, Greenspan appears as *pathologically* skittish. Always doubt the bad news, always fear the good news: that appears to be the fundamental psychology of the man.

And that, in turn, raises the real mystery. How exactly was it that Alan Greenspan, the world's most excessively cautious person, became the first Chairman of the Federal Reserve ever to achieve the 1978 Humphrey-Hawkins mandate of 'full employment, balanced growth, and reasonable price stability'?

Part of the answer appears to be: he met a good woman. Or more precisely, two of them. They were Clinton appointees Janet Yellen and, especially, Alice Rivlin, who came to the Federal Reserve Board in early 1996. Together, Yellen and Rivlin seem to have softened Greenspan, one might even say to have relaxed him, and *without threatening him* as previous monetary doves had done. Having read Martin on Greenspan's intellectual openness to women (in his Ayn Rand days and also later on) one is tempted to see in these postings an ultimate expression of Bill Clinton's psycho-political genius. Or perhaps the President just got lucky.

And the world did change. The Fed adopted a do-nothing policy that held for nearly four years. Checkpoint Greenspan, the toll booth on the road to full employment, shut down. Unemployment fell continuously. Employment rose continuously. Credit expanded to companies and to households; homeownership reached 70 percent of families. Inflation did not rise. The NAIRU died an unmourned intellectual death. Greenspan himself became an icon – the visible architect of the most liberal and humane aspect of the time, a prosperous and inclusive economy in which jobs really did become available to all.

And yet, did he learn from this? There is little evidence that he did. Although Greenspan dropped the NAIRU and flirted with 'New Economy' mumbo-jumbo – the idea that computers, or the Internet, were driving up physical productivity in some way unseen by government statisticians – he never drew the two fundamental conclusions that the situation demanded.

The first is that full employment is benign, something not to be feared but proud of, something to value and to defend. With full employment, social problems of all kinds – crime, stress, ill-health, family break-up, welfare dependency – recede dramatically. Moreover, as we learned in 1999, full employment accelerates productivity growth, so that high rates of growth tend to pay for themselves, for a while. *Full employment is, therefore, worth running risks for.* Yet it remains on the contrary, for Greenspan and his colleagues, a *risky condition* – one that justifies 'pre-emptive' increases in interest rates in order to slow the economy down. Such increases began in 1999, culminated in May 2000, and are being felt very painfully today. They also did untold damage to Al Gore in the election.

The second big lesson is that the big dangers lie not in inflation but in *speculation* – in stock markets, in foreign exchange markets and in external debt. It is not the misbehavior of workers we should fear, but of *capitalists*. Destabilizing financial speculation can be tamed only by powerful regulation. Greenspan and his colleagues had that power – in particular, they could have raised margin requirements on their own. Greenspan could also have lent his authority to stronger efforts by the Administration and Congress to control banking excesses and to stabilize the international financial system.

Instead he did nothing. After 1998, with capital fleeing Asia for American shores, the old Objectivist let the tech boom develop into a huge financial bubble. Margin lending exploded. There followed the enormous enrichment of a tiny Internet elite and the much larger financial one. And after the bubble, came the crash.

For all Woodward's narrative talents, he misses this story. In technical matters, critical capacity and distance are needed; Woodward brings neither to bear here. Indeed, he closes on an note of anticipatory apologetics, one that seeks to excuse our hero from responsibility for the economic slowdown now gathering force. Woodward asks, of Greenspan, 'When would he goof? What was the hidden factor or brewing crisis that no one was anticipating?' The possibility that Greenspan *had already goofed*, with entirely predictable consequences that are now unfolding, does not enter his mind.

(*The American Prospect*, 29 January 2001)

The Man Who Stayed Too Long

Alan Greenspan plays the role of economist, on TV especially, better than any public official who ever lived. But that doesn't mean he is one.

Here is a man who spent the first half of his central-banking career fighting an inflation that did not exist. In so doing, the Chairman of the Federal Reserve triggered the stock market crash of 1987, the recession of 1990–1991 and a 'pre-emptive strike' on the dead beast in 1994. He had one period of glory, the late 1990s, when by doing nothing for four years he managed to bring on full employment without inflation. This was against the almost-unanimous received wisdom of the 'real' economists, it should be said, and for this Greenspan should always be honored.

But then he blew it. He knew that the Internet bubble was getting out of hand. He held the power to do something about it without raising interest rates, but he declined to act. Let me quote myself here, speaking at the White House Conference on the New Economy in early April 2000:

> For its part, and instead of setting off to fight an inflation that is a pure product of academic imaginations, the Federal Reserve Board could control margin lending. Raising margin requirements is the direct approach to a stock bubble, more targeted than raising interest rates and more effective than jawboning the lenders. If a crash comes, sooner or later, a failure to have acted on margins will weigh on the record, and not for the first time.

Instead, just before and even after the Internet crash, Greenspan raised interest rates – unsettling the markets and hitting hard at

Presidential candidate Al Gore. It was the wrong policy, attacking an inflation for which by then not a shred of evidence remained. And then, as the markets tumbled, Greenspan did nothing for six months. Only in December – just as George W. Bush was anointed – did he begin to cut rates. And while that surely helped soften the slump, allowing consumers to continue to borrow and spend through the Bush years, it came too late to save the 'New Economy' from a fiasco costing millions of jobs.

Greenspan has done two other key favors for Team Bush. In 2001, he famously spoke against his own convictions, expressed privately to Treasury Secretary Paul O'Neill, that without triggers making them conditional on the vanishing surplus, the Bush tax cuts were 'irresponsible'. (Now he denies having said this, but there is no reason to believe him.) And in recent weeks he has tried to slit the throat of the Social Security program, calling for benefit cuts while supporting making Bush's tax cuts permanent. John Edwards correctly called this an 'outrage' at the time, and John Kerry said, 'We're simply not going to do it.' But Greenspan is a stalking-horse for the next term of President Bush.

Chairman of the Board of Governors of the Federal Reserve System is truly a wonderful job. Not only is it at the center of power, money, prestige and mystery, but the occupant can do no wrong. He is always praised for the good times, never blamed for the disasters. Nowhere else in American public life is there a position so similar to that of the pope. Or, perhaps, to the president of Mexico, back in the old days: a high priest while in office – and a complete nonentity as soon as the sash is removed.

Greenspan knows this, of course. For what other reason would he, at 78, choose to linger on in his marble palace? He has survived, after all, the Internet bubble and crash, and four years of stagnation since then. We are in that brief, happy moment that follows the onset of war and that often precedes elections: the country's growth rate is fairly high, and even employment has been rising these past two months. Now, for the first time since Greenspan was last reappointed in 2000, retirement would not imply admission of defeat.

Not only this, but the future isn't rosy. High oil and gas prices are percolating through our structure of costs, generating low-grade but perceptible systemic inflation. The dollar continues to fall against the euro. Meanwhile, China is quite sensibly converting some of its dollars into a strategic petroleum reserve. This and other stockpiling will work to keep oil prices up (always allowing for that promised gift from the

Saudis of a few months' price cut just before the election) while further driving the dollar down.

Greenspan is already telling us, as clearly as he ever does, that the Fed will shortly repeat the mistakes of the last oil price shock, back in the 1970s. Faced with inflation – even just a small amount – it will raise interest rates. This is called 'fighting inflation'. The headline writers will say so endlessly, until you almost think it is true. But the effect is just the reverse. As higher rates drain funds from many companies, they will respond by raising their prices even more. Only much later, when the effect of high interest rates is to clobber demand, growth, employment and commodity prices, will inflation finally decrease.

Stock prices rose in 2003 in part because the dollar was falling. Hence US transnational corporations could convert their euro earnings into more dollars, making their earnings look terrific. (No doubt, the Administration's cutting the tax rate on dividends also helped.) A rise in rates and the dollar will unravel this effect. And higher rates may also hit the banking sector, depreciating banks' assets (including mortgage-backed securities) while increasing their costs. Will banks respond, as they did in 1994, by increasing their lending? It's doubtful: pent-up demand for new loans does not appear to be there, as it was 10 years ago.

The outlook, therefore, isn't for another noninflationary boom. It's for stagflation – the combination of low performance and rising prices some of us dimly remember from the Vietnam War. Thanks to Iraq and his own longevity, Greenspan is now likely to go out on a sour note: the man who stayed too long.

(*Salon*, 20 May 2004)

Bernankenstein's Monster

From Alan Greenspan to Benjamin Bernanke. The transition at the Federal Reserve is from insider to academic, from man of action to man of ideas. Greenspan's PhD was awarded by New York University in 1977 as a decoration; he didn't do any work for it. Bernanke, on the other hand, has stellar credentials: summa cum laude from Harvard, PhD from MIT, professorship at Princeton. But apart from a few months at the Council of Economic Advisers, Bernanke has never run anything larger than an economics department. Greenspan ran the Fed for 19 years without ever losing a vote.

Bernanke is known as a model professor. He has a careful mind, an open manner, a not-very-partisan disposition. (He helped recruit Paul Krugman to Princeton, after all – did Bush realize this?) He has written about monetary theory for years; his views are known and settled. Thus the transition is also partly from obscure prose and flexible belief to clarity and conviction.

It sounds great. But at least since Mary Shelley, wise voices have warned that academics in the grip of big ideas can be dangerous. There is the awful temptation to test one's views. And if you happen to be Chairman of the Federal Reserve, you're using the entire country as your lab.

Bernanke's big idea is 'inflation targeting' – the notion that the Federal Reserve should set a numerical inflation objective and pursue that over all other goals, raising rates when inflation exceeds the target and cutting them when inflation falls below it. (He coauthored a book on this in 1999; I gave it a harsh review.) This policy would depart from the Fed's legal mandate, which requires it to pursue 'full employment' and 'balanced growth' in addition to 'reasonable price stability'. Bernanke's rule would also force changes in current practice. Though under Greenspan the Fed always cited the threat of inflation when raising interest rates, in fact, it acted for a wide variety of reasons, stated and unstated; one of Greenspan's defining traits was his unwillingness to be pinned down to any simple policy rule.

Sometimes inflation targeting is harmless. In 2002, Bernanke used it to help argue for lower interest rates. He felt that after 9/11 the danger was of deflation, which hurts those with debt, like most homeowners. There was really very little chance of deflation in 2002 (overall wages and prices in advanced industrial countries rarely decline); the real risk was of a financial panic. Targeting helped sell the correct policy – lower interest rates – but since the forecast was spurious the episode was no great proof of Bernanke's theory.

Inflation targeting would be much more dangerous if applied today. Recently we've seen a small spate of inflation, most of which is due to rising oil prices brought on by the war in Iraq, the hurricanes along the Gulf Coast, and plain old speculation. Suppose the Fed were following a 2 percent inflation target and the 'oil shock' pushed overall price increases up to 3 or 4 percent. Should the Fed raise interest rates in response?

First, assume it did. Higher oil prices have two effects: they push up prices, and unless you're an oil company, they hit corporate profits (check out the news from Ford and GM). Higher interest rates also push up prices, and, unless you're a bank, they also hit your profits. The result: stagflation – inflation and rising unemployment at the same time. Raising interest rates after an oil shock was exactly the mistake the Fed made following the OPEC shocks of 1973 and 1979. In recent testimony before Congress, Bernanke tried to escape this trap, pointing out that price increases haven't yet passed from oil into the rest of the economy. So maybe he's for targeting core inflation – price increases with the two 'volatile' components of oil and food taken out. But here's the problem with that: inflation has to start somewhere. Usually it shows up first in sectors where prices are, well, volatile. Only later does it move to sectors like government procurement, where prices change slowly. So if the target is shifted from actual inflation to core inflation, the Fed would be saying, 'We'll fight inflation, but not until it's really entrenched.' And if you wait until then, you've got a serious problem.

So it seems you're damned if you hurry and damned if you delay.

Bernanke, however, believes that targeting would help fight inflation another way: by sending a clear, transparent signal that would affect what economists call 'inflation expectations'. The idea is that workers and businesses don't just wait to react to higher interest rates. Rather, they set wages and prices partly with an eye to the Fed's policy stance, which they can read about in the newspapers or watch on TV. Thus, if they understand that the Fed plans to be a tough inflation fighter, then supposedly they will keep their wages and prices under control, so as to avoid the punishment of higher interest rates that they rightly fear.

This idea has a pedigree, and curiously enough, some of it is German. In arrangements that endured until about a dozen years ago, the Bundesbank negotiated in effect by threat and counterthreat with the largest trade union. If wage demands were too high, then the bankers would raise interest rates.

The Deutschmark would climb, and the metalworkers, who produced much of Germany's exports, would lose competitiveness and their jobs. An atmosphere of credible threat, in other words, helped keep the workers in line.

But the German system worked (for as long as it did) because the union making the key wage decision also had the most to lose. Higher interest rates, as they affected the exchange rate and foreign trade, would hit them hardest and first. By moderating wage demands, they could keep Germany competitive and prosperous as a whole, and also keep their jobs. So they had something to gain by making a disciplined choice.

In the United States, we don't have a centralized bargaining process, with a strategic union faced off against the central bank. Here the signal would have to be transmitted by the central bank to the public mainly through the press, and implemented in very decentralized labor markets.

I fear I had some small hand in this idea. Thirty years ago, as a young staffer on the House Banking Committee, I organized the first regular hearings on the conduct of monetary policy – what later became the Humphrey-Hawkins process – in which the Fed chair comes before Congress every six months. Before the H-H hearings, the Fed never wanted to speak to the American people. The chairman was typically an ineloquent bureaucrat whose name the public hardly knew. Fed governorships were sinecures. The Humphrey-Hawkins hearings started as a way for Congress to open things up, against vigorous resistance. They have since become a national theater of which the chairman is invariably the star. They have given the Federal Reserve a public presence that would have astounded central bankers anywhere in the world a generation ago.

As a result, both monetary policy and the Fed chairmen themselves are of a higher caliber than when I was a boy economist. (Arthur Burns, the first one I had to deal with, was insecure and a bit of a bully.) Federal Reserve governors – the other members of the board – are also better, and the Federal Open Market Committee, which decides interest-rate changes, has become a place for serious people. I'd like to build on this progress by putting the FOMC meetings on live TV. (Fed-Span, how about it?)

But even such transparency wouldn't mean that the public would come to think and act just as the Fed chairman might like. First of all, the general public is busy; people do not waste that much time following the economic news. But even if they did, rational workers wouldn't heed the Fed's signal. Everyone is always better off, individually, taking a wage increase than forgoing it, for then the cost of a tight policy is shifted to someone else.

There is, in other words, a fatal lack of solidarity in our system. And do oil companies – which recently posted record profits on the strength of record prices – care about the threat of higher interest rates? Of course not. They know that burden will hit elsewhere: on businesses planning investments, on households deciding whether to buy a new house or a new car. What would oil companies fear? Sales from the strategic reserve, mandatory conservation, a windfall profits tax, even (gasp!) price ceilings to curb speculation. Not to worry, though, Bush won't do any of that.

Thus, in the face of an oil price shock, raising interest rates to counter inflation doesn't make sense. It doesn't make sense to do it immediately (as Greenspan has been doing) because that adds to the inflation. It doesn't make sense to do it later, unless you're prepared to put the economy through a recession in order to 'wring inflation out of the system'. And it doesn't make sense to do it as a signal because everyone who can run the red light will do so.

Of late, oil prices have begun to fall, so this all might seem academic. But oil supply shocks are likely to revisit us with greater and greater frequency. And so Dr Bernankenstein has a problem. He can unleash his monster, drive up interest rates, and make things worse. Or he can stand down, demonstrating to instant critics that he lacks the courage of his convictions.

How Bernanke manages such dilemmas will probably determine his fate. As a former professor appointed by a failing President, he hasn't got a lot of ready-made mystique. He may feel pressured to implement his pet theory to prove that he is brave and decisive. But that's a mug's game. If you need to prove it, then you aren't. What Bernanke really needs to prove is that he doesn't have anything to prove. And it may be that the key to showing character, spine, and judgment – all those good things – will lie in not following through on his ideas. Indeed, the path of true wisdom may require finding a creative excuse to do nothing at all.

(Published as 'Ego Inflation'. *Mother Jones*, January–February 2006)

About the Economy

I Don't Want To Talk About It

'Americans Discuss Social Security'. That's the name of a forum being held around the country and in Austin on April 18. Co-sponsored by the Pew Charitable Trusts and locally by my own LBJ School of Public Affairs, the event is part of a national campaign to air options for Social Security 'reform' before local opinion-makers and media markets. If you live and breathe in this country, you've seen the advertising. I won't be in town, so here's what I have to say.

There is no Social Security crisis. Robert Eisner, a past president of the American Economics Association, has written with clear authority on this point:

> The myths about Social Security are perhaps the worst of all the deficit scare stories. They frighten millions of elderly and millions more who hope someday to be elderly. They offer cover for insidious efforts to diminish or destroy a system of social insurance that has served its purpose well for six decades.

Social Security is not 'underfunded'. It is not, in fact, possible to pre-fund Social Security. Tomorrow's Social Security will be paid by tomorrow's workers, out of tomorrow's national product, according to benefit schedules set by law at that time. Those trust funds are just an accounting device, wipe them out and nothing would happen; today's surpluses are just as irrelevant, in economic terms, as tomorrow's deficits. Regressive payroll taxes today buy jet fighters and aircraft carriers. It would not be a bad thing if, twenty years from now, some progressive income taxes were used to pay for pensions.

But anyway, those deficits projected for 2019 are based on pessimistic forecasts; writing in the latest *American Prospect* Robert Reich, who as Labor Secretary was a trustee of the system, calls them 'wildly pessimistic'. Substitute realistic assumptions (for instance, 2.4 percent annual economic growth instead of 1.8 between now and then), and the future deficits disappear, without any cuts in benefits or increases in taxes. Or, if you like, credit the trust funds with a bit of income tax revenue, as Eisner has proposed, and take care of the so-called problem that way.

Yes, we can afford Social Security. In thirty years time, there will be more older Americans to support, but fewer children. Productivity per worker, at present trends, will be as much as 40 percent higher than today. Given our wealth and prospects, we should be talking about how to expand our social protections, about how to make future retirements more comfortable – not about how to cut them back.

Cuts in benefits and higher taxes are both unnecessary. But benefit cuts will affect the living standards of the elderly in the future. Social Security, today, does protect most old people from poverty. If retirement ages go up, or if indexing to the cost of living is scaled back, or if the system is partly privatized so that present features favoring low-income workers are lost, then there will be more poverty among the old.

Who favors such cutbacks? The main supporters are investment bankers and fund managers, who want Americans to rely even more on private retirement savings than they presently do. Divert Social Security payroll taxes into mutual funds, and guess who skims the cash flow? Do you want to understand the politics of Social Security 'reform'? Just remember where politicians of both parties turn for cash.

The stock market is not a better choice. If you compute the return on payroll taxes as though they were an investment, Social Security is a good deal for most workers. It is true that past stock market returns have been high, and that for some upper-income workers stock investments since maybe 1980 would have done better. But there is a contradiction in arguments that project this advantage forward. Past market returns are associated with past economic performance. If the predictions of woe underlying projected Social Security cash shortfalls come true, past stock market returns cannot continue. On the other hand, if the economy performs well enough to support stock gains at past rates, there will be no shortfall in the Social Security funds.

Chile's system is a lousy alternative. Chile's privatized system is inefficient, truly underfunded, and will require large unbudgeted payments to meet poverty-level minimum pension obligations when today's Chilean workers retire. Unlike private mutual funds, which must advertise, compete for accounts (even though they all offer basically identical returns) and pay high-priced managers, the American Social Security System operates efficiently, without frills, and at a tiny administrative cost when compared to privately-managed funds.

In sum: privatization is a bad idea. Raising the retirement age is a bad idea. Means tests are a bad idea. Raising taxes is a bad idea. Cutting benefits is a bad idea. If that's the agenda for Social Security 'reform', I don't wanna talk about it, and you shouldn't either.

There are, in fact, only four things Americans today can do to assure a healthy, prosperous retirement for Americans twenty years from now. We can fight for a full-employment, high-growth economy. We can let in more hard-working immigrants. We can have more babies. As an economist, husband of an immigrant, and father-one-more-time, I'm doing my bit. The fourth thing is to fight off the investment bankers, fund managers, privatizers and crisis-mongers who are spreading false alarms, scare stories and myths about the future of the Social Security system. That much, I'll leave up to you.

(*The Texas Observer*, 24 April 1998)

The Sorcerer's Apprentices

Once upon a time two professors – we can call them Scholes and Merton – got bored with their jobs. They were economists, theorists of finance. Brilliant and accomplished, they were celebrated, even renowned; each would win a Nobel Prize. But it wasn't enough. Scholes and Merton wanted to be very, very rich.

So Scholes and Merton joined forces with Meriwether, a broken-out ex-bond trader and anti-hero of Michael Lewis's *Liar's Poker*, and Mullins, once the Vice Chair of the Federal Reserve Board, to form the storied firm of Long Term Capital Management.

LTCM was a hedge fund. It bought bonds and other debt instruments, and then – using Scholes's and Merton's theories – it packaged and sold equivalent instruments to other financial institutions. This is called hedging.

Hedging is like making money on rounding error. You earn only a little bit on each sale, but make it up with volume. LTCM had capital of $5 billion, at its peak. To get the big volume, it borrowed huge sums – more than $100 billion and by one report up to $1.2 trillion – from banks. This is called leverage. Leverage and hedging – for a long time, they worked like a charm.

But, contrary to the theories of Scholes and Merton, nothing works forever. And LTCM ran, it seems, into two kinds of trouble. First, imitators joined the market, so the opportunities for hedging declined. To make the same money on any given deal, volumes had to go up and up. Second, it seems that LTCM started taking some of its huge bank loans into other fields: for instance mortgage-backed securities and Russian debt. These were old-fashioned speculations where it is much easier to lose your shirt.

162

Last summer, the shirt-losing started. Global capital flooded into short-term Treasury paper, destroying the traditional relationships on which mortgage-backed security speculations depended. Apparently LTCM thought short-term interest rates would rise, but they didn't. And then Russia defaulted; an event the speculators did not think would ever happen.

Now, when a company with 20-to-1 leverage suffers even a 5 percent loss, that's called bankruptcy. LTCM – whose actual leverage may have been higher – was coming close. Banks, to protect themselves, demanded more collateral, or margin. So the company was going to be forced to sell its paper assets, to 'unwind its positions'. The effect might have been to crash the financial markets, with a risk of wiping out the equity not only of the fund itself, but also of the banks that have lent the money and many other people besides.

And so the great gurus of efficient and free capital markets, Merton and Scholes and Meriwether and Mullins, ended up, hat-in-hand, on the government's doorstep. The Federal Reserve Bank of New York convened the bankers, and in effect ordered them to pony up $3.5 billion in new capital, taking over 90 percent of LTCM.

Why did the Fed get involved? Because of a threat to the banking system. LTCM's own money – that $5 billion in equity capital that all but disappeared between July and September – was no one's concern but Meriwether, Mullins, Merton and Scholes (and their partners). But the bank loans they got were your deposits. And a collapse of the banking system threatens us all.

It may be that Alan Greenspan's sudden and forceful appearance before the Senate Budget Committee on September 23, which he requested and which drove up the market by nearly 300 points, was prompted by the looming financial crisis. Nothing like a financial crisis to finally get interest rates down.

Lessons from this fiasco? First, the banks that lent to LTCM were grossly misusing their assets and abusing their responsibilities – something that bankers do all the time and often get away with. It may turn out that the private investors in LTCM were in fact the leaders of the big banks and brokerages, who piggybacked their depositors' money on their own speculations, in which case we have not only a crisis but also a scandal. Much stricter regulation of lending is clearly necessary – though we probably won't get it, unfortunately, so long as bankers dominate the Federal Reserve and investment bankers dominate the US Treasury Department.

Second, we need a major expansion of registration, licensing and dis-closure rules affecting leveraged hedge funds and their relationship to deposit-insured banks. Any operation big enough to threaten the financial markets and to bring the Federal Reserve into action is big enough to operate in the sunshine.

Third, if it turns out that the Federal Reserve itself is indirectly sup-porting this bail-out with public money – for instance with guarantees or by making new loans to the bankers through its discount window – then the public and not the banks should be in charge of LTCM's oper-ations and in control of its positions, and those of any other fund sim-ilarly bailed out.

Fourth, we are going to need a new architecture of global finance – one that stabilizes international currency and debt markets, reduces speculative opportunities, and returns banks to the traditional work of funding commerce and industry. This is the large task that awaits; it will not go away.

And finally, back to Merton and Scholes. Those Nobel prizewinners will now and forever be remembered for the LTCM crisis. They will be remembered for having tried and destroyed, completely, utterly and beyond any redemption, their own theories. That, to this economist, is the great story behind this story.

(*The Texas Observer*, October 1998)

Is the New Economy Rewriting the Rules?

Mr President, the question before this panel is, in effect, 'Can Full Employment Without Inflation Endure?'

According to the 'old rules' and those who believe them, the expansion will not last. Growth is too rapid, unemployment too low, stocks too high. There are deep and mysterious reasons why wage inflation is sure to explode, someday soon. Even more mysteriously, some have even suggested that the rate of productivity growth is too fast.

A second view holds that the New Economy has changed the rules, cutting costs and creating opportunities that never existed before. In part, this is surely correct. The new technologies are today contributing 8 percent of employment and about 35 percent of growth, the Commerce Department reports. They are important, but they are not the whole story.

The third position is that the old rules were wrong, all along. This viewpoint, which I hold, is that for the first time in 30 years we are now seeing the fruits of full employment.

Many economists have lived for decades in fear of full employment. They imagined hidden terrors, like runaway inflation. They did not sufficiently listen to those few, like the great Robert Eisner, who taught that the real rules weren't so grim. Eisner taught that growth could raise wages and yet also spur investment and productivity – in effect that full employment in the Old Economy would bring the New Economy to life.

Mr President, the historic merit of your Administration – and of Mr Greenspan – was to put this proposition to the test. And now we know. In every year since 1993, unemployment has fallen and real growth has exceeded speed limits widely announced in advance. In almost every year, productivity has accelerated. Now we know.

Many also fret that today's prosperity was purchased by high inequality, and particularly that information technologies are inequality producers. But in fact, since unemployment fell below 6 percent, pay gaps have narrowed. Improvements so far are modest. Still, the movement is in the right direction. Today we know that rising pay inequalities are not a price of progress, nor are they a social cost of full employment.

Let us therefore set aside shop-worn worries and the self-immolating doctrine of the pre-emptive strike. If there is a ceiling for growth, or a floor for unemployment, or a limit to this expansion, the truth is that no one knows where they are. Why borrow trouble? Why not take a positive view? Full employment and strong growth are great achievements. Let us celebrate and defend them. Let no one say that the unemployment rate is too low. And especially, let no one say that the productivity growth rate is too high.

Are there dangers? Yes. Inflation, apart from oil prices, is not one of them.

High interest rates are a danger. American households have too much debt. They will become vulnerable when interest rates rise.

Stock market speculation is a danger. Margin lending especially is exploding, and those loans will be exposed if stock prices decline. Some of that is already happening; rising interest rates and speculation on credit are an explosive mixture.

In my view, excessive budget surpluses may also come in time to pose a danger. Too much taxation and too little public spending weaken private disposable income; economists used to call this 'fiscal drag'. For this reason, I do not favor rapid reduction of the public debt for its own sake.

Can the dangers be managed? Yes, they can.

We can offset household debt burdens – and the declining personal savings rate – by raising wages and family incomes. We should raise the minimum wage, expand the EITC as proposed, and support collective bargaining. On average, earnings should keep pace with productivity – a bit more at the bottom, a bit less at the top. We should also modestly expand public services – education and health care and the environment, I would urge, rather than defense – and even consider modest tax relief, carefully targeted and carefully timed.

For its part, and instead of setting off to fight an inflation that is a pure product of academic imaginations, the Federal Reserve Board could control margin lending. Raising margin requirements is the direct approach to a stock bubble, more targeted than raising interest rates and more effective than jawboning the lenders. If a crash comes, sooner or later, a failure to have acted on margins will weigh on the record, and not for the first time.

But a crash need not come. Despite the nervousness of the markets, these are good times. With the right leadership, with prudent policy changes when they are needed, and with cooperation from all branches of government, they can endure. We can continue to grow and prosper, to enjoy full employment and strong productivity growth and a rapidly expanding New Economy. Not forever. But for years into the future – another four, another eight – yes, we can do that. And we should.

(Remarks at the White House Conference on the New Economy, 5 April 2000. This short speech suffered from one drafting defect. The word 'crash' appears to refer to the stock market, which did crash within a few days. I was however thinking of the possibilities for sustaining full employment prosperity, whatever might happen to be NASDAQ.)

So Long, Wealth Effect

Friday's crack in the NASDAQ, a 10 percent drop on top of 20 and no end in sight, should put an end to talk about an inflationary wealth effect. No wealth. No effect.

But what was the wealth effect, anyway? In that bizarre speech at Boston College on March 6, Alan Greenspan put it this way:

> a rise in structural productivity growth, not surprisingly, fosters higher expectations for long-term corporate earnings. These higher expectations, in turn, not only spur business investment but also increase stock prices and the market value of assets held by households, creating additional purchasing power for which no additional goods or services have yet been produced.

Taken literally this was purest nonsense. Productivity growth, reflecting past gains in technology and business organization, has no effect on expectations for future corporate earnings. Higher profit expectations cannot increase stock prices unless funds to purchase stocks are shifted out of consumption, or else borrowed from banks and brokers. And higher stock valuations have little effect on the current consumption of ordinary American households, since the stock holdings of the bottom 90 percent remain minor and half of all households own no stock at all.

But one should not dismiss Mr Greenspan so abruptly. When he speaks in tongues, he is often speaking of something else entirely and perhaps of something not so easily spoken of. Is there perhaps something else to the 'wealth effect'?

Of course! And we all know what it is, including several readers of this column who tried to persuade me, after my last jeremiad, that 'inflation is everywhere' in this economy. (Everywhere, I replied, but in the Chairman's speeches.) Most of them, I noticed, lived near to Silicon Valley.

The wealth effect is – the tech sector. It is, or was, the NASDAQ bubble. It is, or was, the dot-com craze and the mechanism of the IPO.

How so? Simple. Consider the famous Internet model of business operations: Raise capital. Burn it. Grow your company. Cut costs. Go down the learning curve. Realize economies of scale. Drive your competition into the ground. And eventually, at the end of the rainbow, in the sweet hereafter, but not today or tomorrow, make an actual profit on actual sales. How many tech companies have been doing that in the past few years?

Many of them. The circumstances required it. Capital was cheap to raise, profits hard to come by. If you didn't burn, if you didn't grow, you would neither make a profit nor survive to fight another round.

And yet, every one of these companies met a payroll. And all their workers, all their managers, all their engineers and programmers and all of their families contributed to the great stream of spending that has made for the long boom. They were, in effect, converting enthusiastic investment into consumption expenditure through the mechanism of rising valuations. A wealth effect, if ever you saw one.

This wealth effect was charming. In contrast to past frenzies, in real estate or oil, this one enriched the nerds of American folk culture. It fostered a mass of amusing new products. And it promised, with eternal optimism, to change the way we all lived for the better – a promise that was nice to hear even if it was rarely clear just how a search engine or a digital pager could actually accomplish any such thing.

And now it's coming to an end. Over six to eight months the bubble accelerated the financial demands on the New Economy far beyond the capacity of the companies to deliver. More money came in than the sector could handle. Suddenly, promises that might have matured over years (maybe) came due in months. The steady optimists among investors were elbowed aside, the rush took over, and the boom was doomed.

This didn't have to happen. It wasn't inevitable. It was the perfectly predictable product of Mr Greenspan's indifference to speculation on margin, combined with his colleagues' feckless pursuit of higher interest rates. Feed a bubble. Pop a bubble. Then, 'What, who, me?' This is what we are Fed with. We cannot have discipline so we must have pain.

And so, what does the NASDAQ crash mean? By itself, in the greater scheme of things, not very much. Total employment in the IT sectors is not above 10 million, generously defined. In a good deep slump, with bankruptcies galore, how many jobs will go down? One million? Two?

This would be a shame, but there are 130 million working Americans, most of them in companies that do make a profit. For the same reason that the wealth effect did not produce inflation, even a stiff shakeout will not produce a recession. By itself, the sector is too small.

But notice the qualifier. By itself. The Old Economy is doing fine, but any number of things could go wrong, and quite soon. Fiscal drag (the budget surplus is too big). High interest rates. High oil prices. A squeeze on credit that might come from banks reacting to losses on brokerage loans.

We shall now see whether Mr Greenspan can react to the plain consequences of his own dangerous policies and change them, protecting the rest of us before we follow the tech sector down.

Note

James K. Galbraith warned in February with these words: 'Up and up goes the interest rate . . . Bigger and bigger gets the tech stock bubble, until by now everyone knows it will pop. A fierce sorting out seems on its way.'

(The Street.com, April 2000. Shortly after this piece, The Street.com, itself an artifact of the bubble, dismissed all of its freelance contributors, including me)

Incurable Optimists

In the status hierarchy of my profession, the Wall Street economist holds a strangely prominent role. Typically, though not always, he lacks academic standing, analytical achievement, significant publication. Research is foreign to him; independent thought unknown. His job is mainly to get his name into the papers. At this he works exceptionally hard. And the financial pages, which in their turn exist mainly to celebrate the great financial houses, oblige. Hence the Wall Street economist has the luxury of seeing his thoughts in print, without the burden of actually ... well, of actually thinking.

This tribe, a year ago, was predicting up to 3 percent growth for 2001. They now concede that, yes, sorry to say, the economy has slowed. But, one reads, 'no one saw this recession coming'. And so, of course, none can blame the Wall Street economist for failing to warn of the trouble we are in. Moreover, in joyful chorus these roosters today crow in the dawn. Recovery, everyone agrees, is on the horizon for early next year. And so, while a few more tax cuts for business would be nice, thank you very much – nothing very serious need be done.

Notice the fine logic. We cannot cite a forecast for error if everyone made the mistake.

And yet, the fact that we have consensus today validates the present forecast. If recovery fails to develop, in part because of failure to act effectively now, the defense will be ready-made. Since no one foresaw that a recovery would *not* occur, again they will say that no one can be blamed.

But the claim of zero past foresight is actually false. It was possible to predict the present disaster, if not its timing, on simple grounds. Let me demonstrate this, at risk of nesting a quote within a quote, from a so-far-unpublished column written early this fall:

The jump in joblessness is brutal news for working Americans, for investors, for politicians of both parties – and also for many economists.

Last spring, forecasters were optimistic. We were told that the economy might recover in a 'V' – or a 'U' – or in the worst possible case, an 'L'. But there is no letter, in the Roman alphabet anyway, to describe the pattern we are actually observing (though Hebrew has the Vav 'ן' which is pretty good).

By late summer, we were grasping at straws. Perhaps interest rate cuts would save us. Or the rebates. Or lower oil prices. Or a consumer rebound. It didn't happen. Now, the jobless surge has cut sharply against these illusions.

Like most Democrats, I'm tempted by a simple tale: things were wonderful, and then the Republicans screwed up. But in truth this slump should be blamed in part on the Robert Rubin-Larry Summers *Democratic* policy of debt reduction at all costs – on what economists used to call 'fiscal drag,' against which a few of us were already warning two years ago.

Let me quote my review of the *Economic Report of the President* for 1999:

> 'The future of fiscal policy ... is written into law. ... [B]udget analysts now project vast excesses of tax revenue over public spending, sufficient if sustained nearly to eliminate the public debt within twenty years.
>
> 'How likely is this actually to happen? The [CEA] provides evidence, inadvertently, in a chart showing ... fiscal surpluses since 1945. *In every single case, excepting once during the Korean War, the achievement of budget surplus was followed by a slump, with falling real GDP, rising unemployment, and a return to deficit spending.* As a matter of history, the actual achievement of sustained budget surpluses is unheard-of.
>
> 'Why is this so? The old Keynesian answer is *fiscal drag*: the fact that excess taxation and inadequate public spending deplete private incomes and slow down private consumption and investment. This simple phenomenon of yesterday's textbooks has not disappeared. It has, merely, been forgotten, over-ruled by the mass amnesia concerning basic Keynesian principles that seems to afflict the economics profession.'

When taxes go above public spending, public saving is high. But households are crunched, and growth can continue only if private Americans *stop* saving. They did so, completely, and household debts soon mounted to record levels. This could not last forever. And when the Federal Reserve raised interest rates in 1999–2000, that hit the consumer at her vulnerable point.

The recession, in short, not only could be predicted. It *was* predicted. Moreover, given that household debts do not disappear overnight, it could prove long and deep. Recovery early next year is not only uncertain. It is unlikely. The issue now becomes, what to do? My prescription followed after a short rant against Republican tax cuts:

> Democrats should ... focus on their real achievement: full employment without inflation. This is what Americans rightly care about: they want jobs. And if the private sector will not provide jobs or the spending that creates them, then government will have to. Only Democrats, God help us, can make this point.
>
> We need a shortlist of immediate actions. Extend and expand the tax rebates. Expand unemployment insurance and the Earned Income Tax Credit. Enact a prescription drug benefit for seniors – cutting the expense by opening the borders to, ahem, free trade. And raise the minimum wage. None of these actions will likely get through the House or past the White House, but they should be proposed, under a banner reading: Save The Economy First.
>
> And here's one idea that might attract bipartisan support – a slim hedge against disaster. States and localities now buy almost twice as many goods and services as the federal government does. They will cut back massively as their revenues fall. So, why not re-enact general revenue sharing – for Democratic and Republican states alike – and let Washington pay the bills for the teachers, clinics, roads, and renovations that states and cities need? If they have more money than they want to spend, let them rebate *their* sales and property taxes for the next few years.

This column was accepted for publication by the *New York Times*. I sent off the final version to my editor there at midnight on September 10. I wanted it to be on her desk when she arrived for work, at nine the following morning.

(*The Texas Observer*, 21 December 2001)

Enron and the Next Revolution

> It is true, so long as no change of base is made, what is confidently to be looked for is a régime of continued and increasing shame and confusion, hardship and dissension, unemployment and privation, waste and insecurity of person and property – such as the rule of the Vested Interests in business has already made increasingly familiar to all the civilized peoples.
>
> (Thorstein Veblen)

Nowadays there are three classes in America: working people at the bottom, professionals above them, a tiny elite at the top. Democrats represent the professionals, Republicans represent the CEOs. No one, much, speaks for working people, who must rely on the occasional sympathy of leading Democrats for most of the little they get.

Our politics accordingly mirror corporate life, with an opposition out of Dilbert, grumpy but ineffective. Thus, after the 2000 election Democrats abandoned the black voters of Florida, disenfranchised by tens of thousands. In the tax-bill looting that followed, there was just enough grease for the upper middle to buy their silence. Meanwhile raids on work safety, on the public schools, on unions, and the attempt to demolish Social Security fell on the lower orders. In each case, the aim was elite enrichment, amid the indifference of the professional class.

Enron could change that. In details complex, the scandal is essentially simple. A handful of rich men, closely tied to the Texas Republican Party led by George Bush and Phil Gramm, decided to become richer still. Their grand strategy included deregulation of energy, deregulation of derivatives, corrupt accounting practices, overseas tax scams, US diplomatic pressure (delivered by Dick Cheney himself, on India, where Enron had built a white elephant power plant). And then, as the game unwound, they sold their own stock while freezing employee pension accounts. In the end the gang made off with over a billion dollars, that we know of.

Enron's real business was politics. Energy deregulation (written in California especially to the taste of hucksters) helped create the web of commodities in which Enron traded. Derivatives deregulation (courtesy of Gramm and Richard Armey) shielded that market from review.

Consulting contracts to the auditors bought complicity; payments from auditors to politicians fended off the SEC. Enron paid for favors promptly: $100,000 to the Democrats in 1997 to push the Indians around, $25,000 to Texas Governor Perry one day after Enron's Mexico chief got to run the Public Utilities Commission in Texas. Wendy Gramm, who moved smoothly from the CFTC to chair Enron's audit committee, got nearly two million. We still don't know exactly what Enron contributed, in intellectual terms, to Cheney's energy policy, or to Paul O'Neill's defense of overseas tax shelters. But they paid well for it: over time, the big boss George Bush got over $600,000 in Enron cash. That we know of.

Enron reveals, for the first time, just how rot at the top can cut against *professional* interests. Those were not only small fry, but modest millionaires in some cases, who lost their 401(k)s. A professional's pension can't be replaced. And there is nothing a hard-working middle manager fears more, than to end up on Social Security like ordinary folk.

The Administration proudly refused to intervene on Enron's behalf once bankruptcy loomed. But here's the catch. They weren't asked to. *Their* friends had already cashed out by then. Saving the professionals, or the company, was not on anyone's agenda.

White House economist Larry Lindsey (an Enron consultant, $50,000) reviewed the risks of the great bankruptcy to the economy at large. He concluded these were small; he may not be wrong. Most of the direct damage landed on a few thousand people in Houston.

But we shouldn't be entirely sure. Modern corporate America runs on the collaboration of professionals with the elites. In big and small ways, managers, accountants, lawyers and engineers make the system work. In each firm, they have to trust that the big boys are not stealing *from them*. And they control – through their pension funds – vast sums which they must also entrust back to corporate America, through the stock market.

Before 1988, the professionals of Japan also felt that by working and saving, borrowing and investing, everyone would get rich. The crash of that year taught otherwise. The Japanese middle classes felt betrayed, because they were betrayed. Their money, what was left of it, went back under the mattress, where it remains. Japan has not recovered in fourteen years.

Now suppose that American professionals come to feel the same way? The economist Thorstein Veblen, back in the days of Teapot Dome, wrote that the revolution here would not be led by workers.

Rather, revolution could only come to America in the hands of technicians, 'the General Staff of the industrial system', a normally contented
class, 'harmless and docile', in ordinary times. The technicians
however, held the real power. And they might, someday, realize that
the absentee landlords, the vested interests, and their political lackeys,
serve no productive function.

   Enron just might start a chain of events that could, in time, prove
Veblen right.

Note

Quotes from Thorstein Veblen, *The Engineers and the Price System* (New
York: W.B. Huebsch, 1921).

(*The Texas Observer*, 1 February 2002)

Share Revenue, Save Jobs

To the economy, September 11 now appears as a transient shock. Sales, confidence and the stock market plunged, but then returned. The dead cat bounced; optimists declared recovery to be near. The so-called stimulus package died. And so we now face a classic test of the predominant economics. Either recovery will happen, or it won't.

I'm betting against it. For the aftermath of September 11 also boosted the economy in several equally transient ways. Lower interest rates spurred mortgage refinancing. The tax rebates bolstered personal income and saving. Oil prices fell sharply. Good weather extended the building season. And the automakers took heroic losses to clear their inventories, as did retailers at Christmas. All of this, so to say, fanned the embers. None of it provided new fuel.

Meanwhile, larger depressive forces remain in place. Investment continues to fall; unused capacity continues to rise. The automakers are shutting down and laying off. Consumer spending has started to drop. Exports have slumped as recession deepens around the world. Enormous deficits are opening in state and local budgets, with spending cuts or tax increases to come already estimated at near $100 billion for next year. About eight million Americans are jobless now, two and a half million more than a year ago.

Last year's tax cut was supposed to keep America growing. It failed. The Republican goal remains, naturally, to get another tax cut. This is not really economic policy, merely another tactical variation on a permanent agenda. Call it rip-off as a philosophy. Enron writ large.

Democratic strategy has been to help the wounded and hope for the best. Extended unemployment insurance and health care would be useful. But they are not enough. Democrats are having trouble leaving their illusions – budget surpluses, debt reduction, 'fiscal responsibility'. In truth, budget deficits are normal. Right now *large* budget deficits are necessary. The job is to end the recession, to restore full employment, to re-create conditions for growth. If small steps won't achieve this, large ones are demanded.

Alan Greenspan, meanwhile, has lost relevance. He may cut interest rates some more. It won't hurt, but it won't give us recovery either. 'Pushing on a string', they used to call it. Business investment won't return until profits do, and that won't happen until consumers have paid down some of their debts. That will take time. Maybe a lot of time.

What, then, are the choices? Just two.

Temporary, progressive tax cuts may still be considered. One might extend the EITC or roll back payroll taxes for three years – meanwhile freezing the 2001 tax cuts at present levels in order to reimburse the Social Security Trust Fund. This would be useful. But the effect would be limited, by the need of households to raise their savings and reduce their debts. Half of last year's rebates were saved, not spent. Even good tax cuts would now face the same problem.

The other choice is: *increase public spending*. All now agree that spending, in general, is needed. It follows that if households won't, government must. We need spending not just to provide a temporary boost, but to sustain activity until the private sector is ready to spend again. This is the time for schools. Transportation systems. Housing. The environment. For a real energy policy based on conservation and mass transit, cutting our dependence on oil. For a prescription drug benefit. Why not a new home health aide program for seniors? There is work to do. There are people to work. Bring them together!

The most immediate crisis, deserving attention before any other, is in the states and cities. State and local budgets should not be cut. But how to prevent this? By recreating a revenue sharing program for the states, with a pass-through to cities, on a scale sufficient to plug the budget gaps. How much? Let's say a hundred billion in the first year. Pass it very few strings, as a block grant, and get past the Washington gridlock. The Federal Government should also make it easier for states to borrow in support of their capital programs.

This slump may get much worse before it gets any better. Accordingly, we must save ourselves. There is no danger in doing too much. This is not a moment for caution. It is not a moment for faith. It is a moment for action.

Note

In 1975, the author worked on the rescue of New York City for the great Congressman Henry S. Reuss, who knew how, and when, to dare on a grand scale.

(*The Nation*, 11 February 2002)

Hangover in America?

It's the new morning in America, you might say. The President has declared that the 1990s were 'a binge', from which we are suffering 'a hangover'.

What a difference two years makes. As late as mid-2000, no less an authority than Alan Greenspan had a very different view. We were, he wrote back then, living through a technological transformation – some called it a new paradigm – that could permit full employment, balanced growth and low inflation to continue for a long time.

What do we know now?

We know that the tech boom was mainly bubble. Its scientific component was vastly oversold. Huge capital sums were raised, and wasted. Meanwhile, throughout corporate America, profits were overstated under the relentless pressure of the markets. And billions were diverted to the pockets of unscrupulous directors and corrupt CEOs.

Yet though profits were lower than we thought, living standards were actually higher. The 1990s were a good time for American workers, who enjoyed full employment, rising wages, and unprecedented access to credit. Poverty fell during these years, health improved, crime declined, and inequalities in pay (though not income or wealth) diminished. These things, unlike profits, cannot be faked.

Productivity gains in the 1990s were also real. But they were due much more to full employment than to technical change. When labor is tight, businesses find ways to save on labor. But the benefits of these gains did not especially show up in profits, as stock market investors imagined. Instead, they flowed back to households, in lower prices and higher quality – the fruits of competition. As such, productivity gains contributed not so much to profits as to rising living standards without inflationary pressure.

All this was wonderful The problem was only that this prosperity could not be sustained. The bubble, which Mr Greenspan failed to discourage (by raising margin requirements) when he had the chance, was bound to burst. Meanwhile, broader growth was fueled by rising corporate and household debt. From 1997 onward, for the first time in history, Americans ceased saving. Instead they financed spending out of loans – against their homes mainly, and also against their stocks. This too could not go on forever, not once asset prices ceased to rise.

The tech bubble popped back in April, 2000. But we are only now learning just how much damage it did – to the prospects for renewed investment, to confidence in corporate accounting, and to confidence in America itself.

By the summer of 2001, it looked as though the boom in household spending was ending. But September 11, in tragic irony, gave America's families a boost. Government spending soared, raising private incomes. The tax cuts were rewritten to include a cash rebate. Interest rates were cut. Oil prices dropped. The automakers slashed prices (which, incredibly, they continue to do). Good weather prolonged the construction season. And so the consumer hung on, bringing us the inventory bounce and the false recovery – ballyhooed by paid optimists on Wall Street – of early 2002.

Here is where the hangover metaphor breaks down. Because we are 'fundamentally strong', Mr Bush tells us, our troubles will pass. (On this, Mr Greenspan claims to agree.) Recovery is under way. And so, the hangover now evident in the markets will be only an unpleasant memory, soon enough.

But in fact, we won't be all right by lunchtime. Consumer finances are getting worse, not better, as debts rise and asset prices fall. All of the 9/11 stimuli have ended, and some (like the oil price) have been reversed. (True, there is strength in housing, which may keep things going for a while yet.) Meanwhile states and localities are in fiscal crisis, and they will be cutting spending and raising taxes all through the coming year.

Capital flowed in after 1997, but it can also flow out – now that a seemingly stable place to go has appeared in dreary, pedestrian, social-democratic Europe. The Almighty Dollar is, it appears, not invincible after all. The falling dollar will further undermine financial markets, raise some import prices, and yet crush developing countries who export to us but buy from the larger world. Long-term benefits, such as higher exports, may not materialize unless we first get serious about rebuilding both our industrial base and the global financial architecture on which stable development relies.

In short, we face major threats: unsustainable private debts, a rising oil price, a confidence crisis, a fiscal crisis at all levels of government, and a falling dollar amid weak export markets. Not a hangover, in other words, in an otherwise healthy organism – but an underlying disease. Call it debt dependence. Or perhaps, 'capital'-ism.

Both parties are in denial. Mr Bush's platitudes about fundamental strength and the need for 'confidence' reveal the emptiness of his recovery program. The Democrats have not escaped from their own rhetoric of years past, according to which they had discovered the one true elixir for perpetual health: 'fiscal responsibility', low interest rates, and an indomitable belief in technological change. It is true, this formula worked in the 1990s. But that does not mean it will work now.

What would work? Only major changes in policy, strongly suited to the actual conditions of the country and the world. The Senate's action on the corporate scandals was a start. Here is a five-step program for what should come next.

1. *Save the cities and the states.* Last week the Governors (many of them loyal Republicans) finally owned up to their problem: a $50 billion shortfall this past year and no-one-yet-knows how much in the year to come. Local government deficits are uncounted, but probably equally big. There is no justification for allowing the cutbacks in schools, health care, roads and transit, and environmental safety. Congress should ride to the rescue, with a revenue sharing block grant to prevent such cuts – and make less necessary the business-killing tax increases that are also sure to occur. (Felix Rohatyn, Treasurer Phil Angelides of California, and Comptroller Carl McCall of New York, assisted by the present author, presented such a proposal to Congressional leaders in February. It's time now to get moving on it.)

2. *Find new ways to help American households.* Enact a prescription drug benefit. Raise the minimum wage. A new round of tax rebates could help. So would expanding the Earned Income Tax Credit. A temporary cut in payroll tax rates, say for three years, would cut the cost of new employment. To make sure the Social Security Trust Funds stay whole, corporate and estate taxes could be credited to the funds to make up the difference.

3. *Freeze and repeal the out-year tax cuts.* The need is for action – necessarily involving larger federal deficits – in the short and medium

term. The US Government remains an excellent credit risk, and we can afford this action. But the federal deficit should not be allowed to rise forever. Thus we can no longer afford Bush's out-year gifts to friends and supporters, in the form of lower income tax rates, and especially the phased repeal of estate taxes – which would, not incidentally, perpetuate the fortunes of so many corporate crooks from the 1980s and 1990s.

4. *Start conserving oil.* This Administration's strategic vision is geared toward controlling world oil supplies. This is a formula, let none doubt it, for *permanent* war. Do we really want this? The only serious alternative is to invest now, *at home*, on a reconstruction of urban, inter-urban and suburban transport systems, using light rail, subways, trains, and every other alternative to gas-guzzling cars and our choked and vulnerable airlines. Such would be a true homeland security program.

5. *Rebuild the global financial system.* The age of the high dollar – of cheap imports and unlimited trade deficits, financed by the world's poor – is ending, or will end soon enough. The system of free global capital markets, in place for thirty years, has failed to produce the development on which our export prosperity, not to mention global peace and security, depends. A rush to the euro would be disastrous for us, yet we cannot afford to raise interest rates to defend the dollar either. And so we need now a new system of international reserve assets and stabilizing control over global capital flow. We must shut down overseas tax havens, impose Tobin taxes on foreign exchange transactions, and more. We have now seen, up close, the devastating consequences of unregulated private power in the capital markets. This should help us understand the complaints of so many other countries in recent years.

A true recovery cannot happen overnight. But it will not happen at all, unless we begin to discuss it now. We can begin by frankly shaking off the illusion that we are OK. The 1990s were a golden *and* a gilded age, but we cannot return to them – and should not want to. And so we must also discard Mr Bush's hangover illusion. For that metaphor implies an invitation, after all, to get ready for the next binge.

(*Washington Post*, 22 July 2002. Published under the headline, 'If this is a hangover, the exuberance was rational')

The Big Fix: the Case for Public Spending

The economy is in trouble. Investment, far below what it was two years ago, shows little sign of revival. Consumer spending, having held up remarkably during the same time, is now more likely to tail off than to accelerate. And while the Federal Government could soon be spending an extra one or two hundred billion dollars on war, otherwise its spending is also in decline.

The Bush team knows all this. And they realize that the President's neck is on the line, if stagnation continues and unemployment rises into 2004.

And so, Keynesian economics (my own native creed) is back. As Keynes stressed, total spending matters – and not who does it or for what purpose. Tax cuts and deficit spending are therefore the agenda; low interest rates seem here to stay. Stimulus is the watchword of the day. It remains only to fill in the details, or so it seems.

But quick-convert Keynesians are unlikely to be good ones. And their programs, based on crude ideas and analogies – for instance to the tax cuts that led to the Reagan boom of 1984 – may prove ineffective today. This is the political danger Bush faces, and one also that any Democratic opponent had better try to understand.

While tax cuts aimed at the middle class might keep their spending going for a time, the President will aim his tax cuts first and foremost at business and the rich. But lowering taxes on profits and capital gains by no means insures that American corporations rev up their investments. They might. But it is a shaky bet, since many companies doubt they can earn the profits that would enable them to benefit from the breaks. If firms do not grow their investments, then their tax cuts will be passed along to shareholders as dividends, or else to executives as salary. In neither case, can we expect the effect on consumption spend-

184

ing to be large. And so, if the Bush tax cuts fail to stimulate investment they won't have much effect on consumption either.

Bush's consumption plan has one main tenet: relying on Alan Greenspan to keep interest rates low, so that households will continue to borrow. But this fix, which has undeniably worked so far, may run out of steam soon. How much more debt will households willingly incur? How much more will banks willingly lend? And, having cut short-term interest rates to the bone, how far can the Federal Reserve bring down long-term interest rates without putting a lethal squeeze on bank balance sheets? Banks make their money, after all, on the spread.

In government, budget slashing at the state and local levels could unleash chaos. State and local governments cut spending or raise taxes by over $100 billion this year. This potential for home-grown disaster seems to have been off the Administration's radar so far.

The Bush strategy is therefore unlikely to generate the growth and profitability required to restart strong business investment, stabilize households and basic government services and bring down unemployment. A war with Iraq would certainly add to spending and to profits. But if Iraq proves to be the puny opponent that the Administration expects, then even that boost will be at best temporary and fairly small.

This opens the way for Bush's opponents to advance a different program. Such a program cannot be built on nostalgia for the Clinton years, with its balanced budgets and booming markets. That bubble has burst once and for all. The current problems, which were not created by Bush alone, must be solved in new ways.

First, Democrats should stand for saving the government that we have. State and local government spending on schools, health care, the environment and core services is deeply needed and universally supported. It is also imperiled. A federal revenue sharing program is the simplest way to save them, though other devices, such as increasing the Medicaid match, would help as well.

Some may complain about the resulting deficits. But they should realize that those deficits already exist. Either they will be dumped on American households, through higher state and local taxes or service cuts. Or the Federal Government, which alone can afford to do so, can assume them for the next few years.

Second, Democrats should support private consumption by working families today by cutting Social Security payroll taxes temporarily. If Congress would refuse permanent repeal of estate taxes, revenue expected from that source could be credited to the Social Security Trust Fund, keeping it more or less whole. What better way to promote fairness, than to recycle accumulated wealth into the retirement system that supports us all?

Third, if the private sector won't invest, let Democrats call for the public sector to take up the slack for a while. For starters, the government should devote resources to solving one of our biggest problems – energy. We need a better-diversified transportation system. We need programs that promote conservation and the development of renewable fuels. And the government can also help by enacting needed social improvements; such as extended unemployment insurance, universal health coverage and a prescription drug benefit.

Such measures – if large and bold enough – would position the Democrats as pro-growth and anti-unemployment in ways that Bush cannot credibly claim to be. But we must also recognize the dangers of our situation, for these affect us as Americans, Democrats and Republicans alike.

The lurking economic danger today is to the dollar. We no longer live in the world of 1969, when the Bretton Woods institutions – notably the exchange-rate system then run by the International Monetary Fund – protected us (up to a point) against the financial excesses of Vietnam. Nor is it still 1981, when then Federal Reserve Chairman Paul Volcker could defend the dollar with double-digit interest rates. Today, interest rates must remain low, but even so our ability to grow (and run big trade deficits) depends on the caprice of global markets. It depends specifically on the willingness of the rest of the world to add to their holding of dollars and dollar debts. This they have done, without fail, for thirty years.

But will they continue? In the face of low interest rates, a flat stock market, deepening Japanese stagnation, debt defaults in Latin America, and perhaps an unpopular war? Or will they start shifting assets out of dollars, adding a dose of devaluation, and perhaps inflation, to our miseries? Will they perhaps turn Europe – with its balanced economy, diversified energy sources and low military spending – into the rising center of world finance? And if that starts to happen, how on earth should we respond?

It's not an easy question. There is certainly no easy answer. But we may need to ponder it, if we hope to enjoy a return to prosperity any time soon.

(*Los Angeles Times*, 29 December 2002)

Bush's Tax Package and Economic Reality

This President gets good press. 'Bush Offers a Cure' was the banner on the *Chicago Sun-Times* on January 8 – to take just one example. Commentators everywhere are calling his 'bold' and 'daring' tax-cut proposals a 'stimulus package' and a 'recovery program'. Even the big number plays well. Six hundred and seventy-four billion! Imagine that.

But in fact, this is not a big program. It is not a 'recovery program'. It isn't much of a 'stimulus package'. That $674 billion is spread over ten years. Only about $100 billion is set to be paid out this year. That's only about 1 percent of economic output this year.

Any tax reduction puts money in the bank. But there isn't an effect on economic growth until consumers and businesses actually go out and spend. Will they do so? Some will. But many businesses already have too much capital equipment they can't use. And households may prefer – initially at least – to pay off some of their enormous debts. For these reasons, Bush's plans will generate even less than $100 billion of new private spending this year – and perhaps, a lot less.

The key element in the Bush plan is the proposal to eliminate federal income taxation on corporate dividends; some $364 billion out of the whole package is due to this one proposal, and $20 billion of the early impact. As an inducement to new spending, this is by far the *least* effective part of the plan. Most dividends earned by middle-class households escape tax already, as they are paid into tax-deferred pension accounts. *Taxable* dividends are paid overwhelmingly to the very rich. Over ten years, more than $75 billion of the loot from Bush's cut will flow to people making more than *one million dollars* a year. Such people don't tie their spending to their incomes.

The dividend proposal would raise the after-tax return on common stocks, relative to bonds. It is therefore an inducement to sell bonds and buy stock. This could push up prices in the stock market, particularly blue chips. No doubt that would generate a lot of cheery headlines – if it works. But the actual effect of this highly artificial price adjustment on business investment and job creation would be very, very small.

The proposal would create a new class of financial instruments – tax-exempt dividend-bearing corporate stock. This is very bad news for state and local governments, who now raise capital by issuing tax-exempt state and municipal bonds. They would face higher financing costs, which means that new schools, roads, parks, museums and libraries will all become more expensive.

A further effect would be on 401(k) plans and individual retirement accounts – the middle class's way of holding stock. Bush's plan would greatly reduce the tax advantage of those plans – making it no less advantageous to hold common stock directly. Discount brokers would emerge as big winners – which may explain why Charles Schwab spoke up for this cut at Waco last fall.

Overall, Bush's new plan fits a pattern: he apparently believes that rich folk should not be taxed. This is true, whether their income takes the form of executive salaries (top income tax rates are also being lowered in the new Bush plan), dividends, capital gains (already tax-favored), or from the estates of their rich aunts and uncles. And as Bush's dream is realized, the tax burden will shift onto working people – whose payroll taxes, notably, are already much higher than income taxes in most cases. Payroll taxes also already cover much more of the Federal Government's daily bills than the Social Security benefits to which they are supposed to be dedicated.

This is why one clear alternative to the Bush tax scheme is to provide a short-term, partial holiday from the payroll tax. This measure would place the new income in the hands of working people who would, almost certainly, spend most of it. A payroll tax holiday on the employer side would also provide direct relief to many labor-intensive small businesses – who need it right now. Social Security, for the moment, *doesn't* need the money. (However, to keep Social Security's finances whole, why not restore the estate tax and dedicate its future revenues to the Trust Fund?)

But there is a better and faster way yet to get new spending. That is for *government itself* to step up spending. Government purchases enter the GDP directly, when they occur; there is no need to wait for households or businesses to decide between saving and spending. For this reason, a war with Iraq, if it costs the $200 billion this year that some experts have estimated – will dwarf the near-term impact of the new Bush tax proposals.

Bush does have a spending program: Ballistic Missile Defense. A new study by Economists Allied for Arms Reduction estimates the full cost of BMD at over one trillion dollars over the next thirty-three years. But like the tax proposals, most of it is irrelevant to the economy right now. Mostly, the fifty to sixty billion dollar annual cost of missile defense in the peak spending years will simply get in the way of other military programs, of needed non-defense programs, and of Social Security. Those big bills for BMD will come due just when the baby boomers get set to retire.

Much better than this policy of rockets and caviar, is the government spending we already have. This is the spending, mainly by state and local governments, on our schools, universities, hospitals, roads, parks, libraries, museums and the environment – not to mention the bill for homeland security which has been largely dumped on cities and states.

As everyone knows, this spending is under siege. Since states and localities have to balance their budgets, and since revenues are crashing, vital services are being lost – just when the larger economy most needs for them, and the jobs and incomes they provide, to be preserved.

Thus, the best single economic measure right now would be a large, temporary new program of federal revenue sharing. That could be coupled to a larger Medicaid match, expanded coverage for unemployment insurance, and other immediate and needed forms of relief.

Bush's plan includes $10 billion for the states. But that is pathetically small: enough to cover estimates of the gap in Texas alone, more or less – or less than one-third of the meltdown in California. Since boldness is being praised these days, let's make an alternative big enough to stop spending cuts by state and local government. A $150 billion program, all told, this year and next, would come closer to meeting the need.

And that could be paid for, over ten years, by *not* enacting Mr Bush's pointless, ineffective and unfair proposal to make corporate dividends tax exempt.

(*Austin American-Statesman*, 12 January 2003)

Cashing Out

In an Uncertain World: Tough Choices from Wall Street to Washington, by Robert E. Rubin and Jacob Weisberg (New York, Random House 2003)

This is a book written entirely in the first person singular voice of Robert Rubin, but to what extent *by* him remains unclear. Jacob Weisberg, editor of *Slate*, is the co-author. But he is not a player in the story; nor is he referenced in the dedication, author's note, or except fleetingly in the acknowledgements.

And though *In an Uncertain World* tells Rubin's life story, it is not a memoir. By his account, Rubin's private life is pleasant, colorless, uneventful; his family has included influential grandfathers, smart children, a patient and supportive wife. He likes to fish; mercifully if he golfs we do not learn of it. When he tells of occasional dealings with unsavory people, such as a Goldman-Sachs partner arrested for insider trading in 1987, he withholds the name. Rubin is evidently a good-humored man. But if he has a sense of humor, this too he conceals.

Rubin built a high reputation in Washington and it is easy to see why. He was good to work for, and he repays subordinates here, notably Larry Summers, Gene Sperling, Caroline Atkinson, Sylvia Mathews and David Dreyer, with unstinting praise. He is respectful to politicos like George Stephanopoulos, going out of his way to mention moments when they were right and he was wrong. He stays cool even when dealing with people who don't deserve it:

> Gingrich was very friendly and so was I. But even after a few years in Washington, I couldn't relate to the idea that shouldn't take it personally when someone calls you a liar and a thief. (p. 176)

Yet this is not an insider's history, such as Sid Blumenthal – that Hieronymus Bosch of our time, Harvard's Richard Parker has called him – has already provided of Clinton's years. It is not a celebrity history, padded with travelogue *à la* Hillary Clinton. It is not a full account of Rubin's own policy interventions. Notably omitted is his role in the repeal of Glass-Steagall, the law that once separated investment from commercial banking. This is a point for which Rubin comes under barbed criticism from Joseph Stiglitz in a new book, *The Roaring Nineties*, and it is curious that Rubin, whose career spans banking of both types, chooses to leave it out.

In an Uncertain World is instead a statement of public philosophy. Its purpose appears mainly to be to impart lessons for economic policy decision-making, and to do so mainly through the prism of several important case studies. These include the Clinton economic plan, the rescue of Mexico in 1995, the Asian financial crisis and the stock market bubble with which the decade ended.

What then are the central lessons? The great Austin ice cream parlor known as Amy's has a motto: 'Life is uncertain. Eat dessert first.' Rubin takes the first half, rejecting the second. His motto, if he had one, might be, 'Life is uncertain. Be careful.' It is good advice, sober and sensible without doubt. And yet it falls curiously short of wisdom.

Rubin came to Washington from Wall Street, and he claims that he knew little of either economics or politics. It is not too difficult to believe. His economic lodestars are fiscal restraint, a high dollar, respect for the judgment of financial markets, deregulation generally and certainly free trade. He seems to have held a mild view of the Republicans in Washington until he had to work with them up close, and even after: in 1994, he writes, 'I didn't begin to foresee the full consequences of a Republican-controlled Congress' (p. 152). Nobody who had worked in Congress would have suffered that problem.

Faced with specific crises, Rubin was pragmatic and willing to take risks as necessary. He pushed for Clinton's tax increases because he knew that spending cuts alone could never do it all. He was prepared to lend Mexico more than it needed, in order to make a credible statement to the financial markets. In the Asian crisis he orchestrated a campaign of support for the IMF that was unpopular on all sides (and rightly so, in many respects).

And yet, missing from these pages is any special insight into Rubin's great problem: how to govern the US and the world economy in our time. Clinton's economic program succeeded, but it led to a bubble and bust from which we have not recovered. Do Rubin's Treasury and

Greenspan's Fed, who stood idly by, bear no responsibility? Rubin thinks they don't. Would the same policies work now? It is unlikely, but one would not learn why from this book.

And while the Mexican rescue also worked, Treasury policies toward Asian liberalization and especially toward Russia were disastrous, leading to economic and human calamity. Rubin blandly passes the buck. Markets 'tend to shine a spotlight on real economic problems' he writes (p. 246). But they don't cause problems. They aren't, and perhaps can't be, inherently unstable. When there is a crisis, it is always because some country out there has failed to 'reform'.

This is belief, not analysis. Rubin has the custodial view of an inside player, who did well in a financial game to which he was happy later to return. He is not a man to challenge the rules. But the times may require that, once in a while. And one may well ask, when the chance next arises, whether someone else like Robert Rubin should again be placed in charge.

(*Washington Post*, 20 November 2003)

Bankers Versus Base

There may come a day, in January 2005, when the Democrats will come back to power. Can we perhaps divert ourselves from the campaign long enough to ask, what then?

The Democrats have a problem. Their base wants jobs and security. Their financial leadership wants a return to the Clinton formula of deficit reduction, leaving low interest rates to generate economic growth and jobs. John Kerry's emerging economic platform pays heavy homage to this formula, but it is unlikely to work out. A return to Bill Clinton's policies will not reproduce Bill Clinton's results. There are at least six reasons why this is so.

First, we are still in the turbulent wake of the technology slump. Capacity utilization remains low, depressing business investment. This overhang will heal eventually, but in most sectors it hasn't healed yet. As a result, private business is not yet poised for another takeoff; don't expect another dot-com bubble real soon.

Second, household debt burdens remain high. Households are therefore unlikely to fuel consumption growth by adding sharply to the debts they already have. More likely, the housing bubble will deflate, slowing rather than accelerating consumer spending in the years ahead.

Third, state and local governments are still cutting back, adding the drag of reduced direct-spending cuts and higher taxes to the economy. This is true even though overall state and local budget deficits have been reduced by drastic measures already taken.

Fourth, assuming growth does not give out on its own, interest rates are more likely to rise than to fall once the election is past. We are feeling the pressure now from Europe and Japan (and from our own 'strong dollar' advocates) to defend the dollar against the euro. Alan

Greenspan, in his oblique but unmistakable way, is already warning that this will happen.

Fifth, our growing structural trade deficit (including the effects of outsourcing) drains increasing US demand overseas even as the economy tries to expand.

Sixth, a climate of fear and apprehension, much aggravated by Team Bush and its war on terrorism, seems to be weighing on the business mind. In such a climate, will companies boldly take new risks, requiring the addition of new employees to the payroll? It appears they won't do it very much – though fits and starts will recur from month to month.

Back in 1992, the big barrier to growth was financial. Banks were recovering from the fiascos of the 1980s and were unwilling to lend. Businesses and households, on the other hand, were very anxious to borrow. We had a 'credit crunch', which Clinton's 1993 budget and Greenspan's monetary policies helped to unstick. After that, the economy grew largely on its own, powered by business optimism and household debt. Today, there is no credit crunch. Our problem is not a shortage of lenders but fear for the future. It is the classic symptom of a creeping depression.

These are the main reasons why job forecasts have been frustrated in the past three years. Economists purport to be surprised about them; we read in the press, repeatedly, that 'no one' predicted it. That's not true. Economists who applied a systematic Keynesian framework to current conditions – notably, Wynne Godley of Cambridge University and the Levy Institute, and this author – have been issuing warnings on these issues since the 1990s.

And so, a strategy of fixing the deficits first-and-only won't work in 2005. Declining deficit forecasts will not ensure stable, low interest rates. And easy money will not suffice to bring us back to full-employment prosperity. More – much more – is going to be needed.

The same factors also work against the quick fix of another short-term 'economic stimulus' program. One hears this old song from the liberal wing of the Clinton coalition, alongside calls for selective tax breaks of various kinds and increased job training. But under the conditions we now live in, short-term measures – though useful – work only in the short run. Once the stimulus ends, the effects do, too. Cases in point: we had a stimulus package in 2001 (rebates) and again in 2003 (child tax credits). After both, growth rates surged but then subsided. (This cycle may be happening again, thanks to large tax refunds being passed around right now.)

As for training, the problem is not a shortage of skills. It is an extreme shortage of good jobs, combined with bad pay and poor working conditions. Apart from some special cases, job training is a feelgood measure; it does not address the real problem.

The task of the new Administration, therefore, will be to set a new direction for growth and jobs, not only for the short term but also over the medium and long term. Tax cuts (even if targeted well) and easy money are likely to contribute little to this objective. Health care reform and education are important, but they probably create few new jobs. We need, in short, a patient strategy for social investment – to meet pressing national objectives while creating jobs, recognizing that success will take determination, time, and money.

What objectives? The foremost candidate is sustainable energy security. Reducing our exposure to the world oil economy is a vast public challenge. It would move us toward compact cities, new transport systems, and renewable energy sources, as well as toward much more conservation and efficiency in the use of oil. That is the sort of national effort that would bring good jobs in quantity to the next generation, leaving our children and grandchildren better prepared to live well – and in peace.

How to pay for it? Of course we must repeal George W. Bush's tax cuts on the wealthy. We should also forthrightly consider tax incentives to reward efficient energy use and to penalize waste. But for a project of national reconstruction and investment, much of the necessary funds can, and properly should be, borrowed. Policy should do what is necessary to restore jobs. Full employment, sustainable development, and national security are proper goals for policy. Deficit reduction, as such, is not. Public debt to enrich the wealthy is one thing. Debt to rebuild the country is something else again. If we have to go that route, we should do it and not look back.

Meanwhile, the right way to display fiscal discipline would be to separate capital from current expenditures in the budget, leaving the former free from any cap. Even over the long run, debt can grow as the country grows. Stabilizing the public deficit at, say, 3 percent of total income may be a reasonable midterm goal – once employment, household finances, and our trade picture have been decently restored. But getting to that point will surely require more borrowing, not less, in the meantime.

The Democratic base and the financiers tend to clash on two other key issues: Social Security and trade. The financiers speak of a looming

Social Security crisis. With this language, they signal a wish to 'fix' the system by reducing benefits or by raising the payroll tax.

But is there a Social Security crisis? Actually, there is not. If the future economy performs even at the average of the past, or if population growth is more rapid (as the US Census Bureau now assumes), the shortfalls disappear.

But suppose they don't. Even then, it's a crisis only if you think that Social Security benefits must always and only be paid from the payroll tax. But why should this be? Such taxes already take too much from the incomes of working households. Apart from raising the earnings cap, higher taxes on a declining base of employed workers would only make their hardship worse, as well as making it more costly for businesses to provide jobs.

So should retirement benefits be cut, directly as Alan Greenspan now advocates or by the subterfuge of privatization? No. Fully two-thirds of elderly Americans rely on Social Security for most of their income. They are not a pampered class and it is not their fault that they are living for a long time.

Here is an obvious solution: if there is a Social Security funding gap, fill it by raising taxes on those who can afford to pay. The right transfer is from the wealthy (some of them elderly), not from the young. How? Restore the estate and gift tax (and perhaps raise the rate on the largest estates). Impose a new top income-tax rate for millionaires. Impose new taxes on financial transactions. Close the loopholes that permit, in particular, the use of offshore tax havens. Revenues from these sources can be credited contingently to the Social Security Trust Fund – to pay benefits if the pessimists are right and new revenues are eventually required. If not, they can go to deficit reduction.

New Social Security taxes may not be necessary. But if they are, both fairness and full-employment economics say that accumulated fortunes should be taxed before adding either to the difficulties of old age for the boomers or the tax burdens of low-wage workers.

Finally, the financiers maintain an unbroken commitment to free trade – part of their enduring love affair with globalization. Here the financiers hold the high ground, because free trade is widely accepted as tantamount to virtue in economics. And outsourcing, though politically potent, is not the primary reason why we've lost more than 2 million jobs under Bush.

There are good reasons to favor open trade. But conditions have to be met for open trade to work. They aren't being met today, and we can change that.

First off, the all-purpose free-trade argument of comparative advantage just isn't very relevant to our trading world. Comparative advantage holds that increased trade raises productive efficiency in both trading partners. But this rests on differences in the technologies deployed by different countries. In modern trade in manufactured goods, technologies tend to be similar wherever found.

A cruder but more relevant argument for trade between North and South – call it the Tom Friedman version – rests on the simple fact that goods and services from poor countries are cheaper. This is not because technologies differ but because of lower wages paid for identical labor, under similar production conditions.

Some Americans do benefit when we purchase software from an Indian who makes $11,000 per year rather than from an American who gets paid five times as much. But does America benefit as a whole? The answer: it depends.

First, does the displaced American worker quickly find a new job at reasonable pay? If so, the loss (of income) is mainly personal. But if the jobs aren't there, the loss is also social – the waste of talent and independence hurts us all.

Second, can we accept the redistributive effect? Part of what one American loses to trade or outsourcing (his or her job and the pay it generated) is usually gained by another American – either the multinational who profits from selling at a lower cost or the consumer who gets a lower price. If the gain goes to profit, as it often does, growing trade raises inequality. If we don't like that, let's have rigorously progressive taxation (and, yes, redistribution) of those gains. This should be a price of trade – and free traders should support it, much more than they do.

Third, the pro-trade, pro-outsourcing case assumes that there is no macro-financial risk. If exports always rose by the exact same amount as when imports rise, there wouldn't be any risk. But increased imports are actually paid for partly by adding to our permanent external debt. This is a short-term benefit. What used to cost, say, $55,000 per year in cash is now had for $11,000 on credit. But how long can it last? At some point, the price may truly be paid with a severe decline of the dollar and falling living standards in the next generation.

All of this suggests that the next Administration ought to make a far more serious commitment, not only to full employment but to adjustment assistance, to progressive taxation, and to more equal wages and salaries – spreading around, in the national interest, the gains from trade.

We should also consider the strategic as well as the equitable aspects of our trading patterns. Why continue to protect such bastions of Republican power and environmental degradation as Florida citrus and sugarcane? And is it really smart to abandon steel, which we will need for national reconstruction and energy security? Why can't a national investment program buy steel from American sources while leaving private steel users free to purchase cheap steel on the world market? If we used a National Interstate and Defense Highways Act to get ourselves into this pickle, why not a National Defense Rail Act to get out?

Perhaps most important, we are going to need a stabilizing reform of the international financial system in the years ahead – a new system that will promote our advanced exports, and the global development process, and therefore help us to better balance our trade. It is not a change that financiers enjoy contemplating, as it will greatly erode their power. But the dollar-credit system is now more than 30 years old; it is unlikely to last another 30 years whatever we do. Our goal ought to be to manage a tolerable transition – better for us, and better for the world, than the alternative of a crack-up. We should start thinking about how to do it, and fairly soon.

The next Democratic Administration will be – as always – a coalition of monied and working interests. But whose interests should predominate? The Clinton formula put the liberal financiers in the driver's seat. Without question, that program worked: it had real costs, but the benefits, while they lasted, were greater.

The problem is that it would be dangerous – to national security, to the retirement security of working Americans, and to the very future of work in this country – to assume that the same formula will work again. In all likelihood it won't.

And it shouldn't be tried, either. It will be better economics, next time, to align policy from the beginning, mainly – though let us hope, carefully – with the interests of working Americans who form the base of the Democratic Party.

(*The American Prospect* online, 4 May 2004)

Keeping It Real for the Voters

AUSTIN, Texas – Surprised though you may be to hear this, the Presidential campaign is just getting started.

Yes, we know the candidates. But what are the real issues? They are not so clear.

And one reason they aren't is our national weakness for the misleading phrase, for the sexy label that somewhat, but imperfectly, covers the case. Herewith a brief guide to what is real and what is not.

- *Jobs, not outsourcing.*   The exodus of manufacturing and software jobs is a hot-button topic. Some small things could be done about it. Adequate enforcement of privacy rights and security interests, for example, would curtail a fair amount of offshore computer programming. But generally speaking, if the Indians want call centers and the Chinese want TV factories, you can't stop them.

  The challenge is to find useful work for all seeking a job here. We still need at least 5 million new jobs. We could start by supporting state and local governments with a revenue-sharing program, and their capital-spending projects with a new federal capital budget and revolving fund. We could add teachers, nurses, firefighters and police to the public payrolls. Let's have an energy and transportation program to rebuild our country for an oil-short world.

  And let's look forward to the day – instead of fearing it – when we'll have a lot more elderly retirees. Who will take care of them? How about a corps of home healthcare assistants? You could create a lot of useful jobs that way.

- *Future deficits, not those right now.*   Those who bemoan the lost surpluses of the late 1990s miss the point. Today's deficits are large, but

199

they are necessary. The private sector will not borrow as it did five years ago, neither for business investment nor for household consumption. So the public sector must borrow, heavily, for the time being. To create enough jobs when we need them, deficits may have to grow for a while.

Are deficits driving up interest rates, crowding out private investment? No. Interest rates at historical lows didn't budge these last few years as both actual deficits and the forecasts got worse. Long-term rates are reacting now – but only to the clear signal that Federal Reserve Chairman Alan Greenspan will soon raise short-term rates.

What about those frightening forecasts of huge deficits? They matter, mainly for a political reason. Given the deficit phobia of our political culture, the government will be unable to address national needs if it doesn't show how future deficits can be brought under control. This is why the back-loaded, top-heavy parts of President Bush's tax cuts should be repealed.

- *Healthcare, not Social Security and Medicare.*   Social Security is in pretty good shape – and will remain so. The drumbeat of Social Security Cassandras has been heard for decades, mainly from people who would like to get their hands on the cash flow. Want to help balance Social Security's future books? Then let's reinstate the estate tax and credit it to the trust fund.

  On the other hand, the cost and waste in our health care system are a travesty. The recent Medicare giveaway to the big drug companies will have to be fixed. We should move toward an efficient, universal health insurance system – and had it not been for politics we already would have.

  But don't pay attention to those who throw around claims that the government is about to go bankrupt over the baby boomers. It isn't. To the contrary, with smart policy, the country can meet its needs and still be much richer in 50 years than it is today.

- *Tax fairness, not tax hikes.*   Bush aimed his tax cuts at the super-wealthy. Taxes on corporate profits have nearly disappeared. Meanwhile, more than 20 years of regressive Social Security payroll taxes have risen and, in the recent budget crisis, states and cities have been hiking their property and sales taxes. Workers, the middle class and the poor pay those. It's a horror that taxes have fallen so much for the very wealthy and risen so much for the working poor and the middle class.

This issue is central to the kind of society we are now and are likely to become. A plutocracy cannot also be a democracy – and the tax code is the way that we choose between them.

- *The dollar, not the renminbi.* There's been a lot of chatter about China's currency manipulations. Of what does that consist? Well, China has pegged the renminbi ... to the dollar. Some manipulation.

  But the dollar is in a lot of trouble. Though the rising euro has been good for our stock market and our exports, the falling dollar is bad for inflation and for our living standards. Watch out after the election. Part of what is driving Greenspan is the urge to defend the dollar, which will mean higher interest rates and probably the end of the credit boom and housing bubble. There is no easy solution to this problem. The hard solution is to rebuild a functioning, development-friendly international financial system. The next President will have to face this issue, even if today's candidates do not.

- *Will the recovery continue? Not: Has it started?* We've got growth. Don't you know there's a war on? Wars always goose total spending and the growth rate.

  But what will happen after the election, when interest rates go up (to 'fight inflation', as they will say) and domestic spending and Social Security and Medicare come under fire? You do not have to be a genius or a depressive to be worried.

- *Iraq.* Misleading labels have bedeviled us in Iraq. Weapons of mass destruction was one, covering a nuclear threat that didn't exist, alongside chemical and biological weapons that wouldn't have amounted to much of a threat even if they had existed. Are we fighting for 'democracy' in Iraq? If so, it will be a long, long war. Will we transfer 'full sovereignty' to the Iraqi government by June 30? Not if that means control over military operations. The 'war on terror' is the worst of the bad labels. It is used to confuse the necessary struggle against Al Qaeda, which actually did attack us, with the ruinous distraction of Saddam Hussein, who was bottled up in Baghdad. The real issue now is: can we find our way out of Iraq, somehow, and still win the fight with Al Qaeda?

Finally, let's note how some of these fungible phrases have moved back and forth between war and economics. In 1994, Greenspan was talking about a 'pre-emptive strike' against inflation – an economic weapon of mass destruction that also did not exist at the time. And we recently learned that for Alberto R. Gonzales, the White House counsel, the 'war on terror' is a 'new paradigm' that justified dismissing the Geneva Convention's absolute prohibition against torture. It seems I remember that latter phrase from the 'New Economy' boom. It was a bad thought in that context, and worse in this.

(*Los Angeles Times*, 27 June 2004)

Dazzle Them with Demographics

The Coming Generational Storm: What You Need to Know About America's Economic Future, Laurence J. Kotlikoff and Scott Burns (Cambridge, MA: MIT Press, 2004)

Laurence Kotlikoff came to Texas in May, to speak to the new graduates in economics and to give a seminar at the department. After hearing him grimly forecast the impending bankruptcy of our government, I asked him why the financial markets hadn't noticed. Uncle Sam is still able to borrow for 20 years at a bit less than 5 percent. How come? Kotlikoff replied that the markets were crazy.

Hubris is alive and well in economics.

The Coming Generational Storm, by Kotlikoff and financial journalist Scott Burns, comes endorsed by liberal and centrist academic economists, including Nobel Prize winners Dan McFadden and George Akerlof, the former chair of Clinton's economic council Janet Yellen, and the financial economist Robert Shiller. The signature blurb, however, is by Peter G. Peterson, Secretary of Commerce in the Nixon Administration and Wall Street's leading Social Security Cassandra ever since. The world long ago ceased listening to Peterson, and he is obviously pleased to have a young ally with such impressive backing. It baffles me that the others could have read this book and still have said what they say.

You think I exaggerate? Read for yourself Kotlikoff's prediction of life in these United States 26 years from now:

> You see major tax evasion, high and rising rates of inflation, a growing underground economy, a rapidly depreciating currency, and more people exiting than entering the country. They're leaving because they're sure things will get still worse. You see political instability, unemployment, labor strikes, high and rising crime rates, record-high interest rates. You see financial markets in ruin. In short, you see America plunging headlong toward third world status.

It's enough to make you pine for the days (not so very long ago) when forecasting fantasists were projecting the Dow at 36,000. At least that mania was optimistic.

And what is the cause of this terrible future? It lies mainly in a terrible, terrible epidemic, no, a scourge, no, a HOLOCAUST of unprotected sex. Sex? Yes, sex. Sex committed in all conjugal respectability by our parents and grandparents beginning 60 years ago, the seeds of doom sown in celebration of victory over Germany and Japan. The baby boom – the original sin, a ticking time bomb, an oncoming freight train, no, a tsunami, no, a KILLER ASTEROID on demographic collision course with planet America. Block that metaphor, as *The New Yorker* used to say.

How is it, then, that Kotlikoff and Burns have uncovered what is unknown to the financial markets, unreported by the government, and previously undiscovered by professional economists – despite the fact that the very last baby boomer came into very well-documented, very well-counted existence almost a half-century back?

The answer is that Kotlikoff has created 'inter-generational accounting'. The essence of this is that receipts must equal commitments over time; the young must plan collectively to support themselves when old, by paying into a fund a sufficient amount to cover their eventual needs, allowing for the time-value of money. Whether this is done by taxes or by 'investing' – by lending now to the government what would otherwise be taxed – is immaterial. The failure to do one or the other supposedly represents a burden on future generations. Kotlikoff's concept of 'fiscal relativity' – which he compares (I'm not kidding) to Einstein – holds that current measures of deficits, saving, and income are meaningless. The only thing that really matters is whether the present values of taxes and spending match.

And when generational accounting is applied to the current commitments of the Federal Government, especially under Social Security and Medicare, some large gaps open up. Kotlikoff and Burns come up with a frightening deficit number: 45 trillion dollars in net present value terms. But what is the meaning of 45 trillion dollars in net present value? Our actual GDP is around 12 trillion dollars a year. So we have a mortgage, of infinite maturity, of between less than four times our current annual income. Does this sound so terribly out of line?

Moreover, the payment schedule is very back-loaded. Social Security is presently in cash surplus, and will be for years to come. The near-term cash 'deficit' of Medicare – that part not covered by the payroll tax – is a mere 1 percent or so of GDP now, and it's intentional.

Medicare was always designed to be funded partly by general revenues, a point that doomsayers about the program determinedly ignore. Projections show the Social-Security-and-Medicare cash deficit (most of it, Medicare) rising above 10 percent of GDP three-quarters of a century from now. But these projections are highly pessimistic, partly because they assume that economic growth will be lower than what we've experienced in past decades. They also assume that medical expenses will continue to rise well above normal inflation rates, until medical costs per person reach four times what they are in every other developed country. This is possible. No doubt given the increased longevity of our seniors (itself a medical triumph), medical costs will rise. But is it likely? Let's hope not.

Even conceding the forecasts, what do they come to? Kotlikoff and Burns claim they will require 'doubling the payroll tax in the short run' (by which they mean by 2030) and tripling it by 2075. This ignores the possibility that other taxes – for instance on income or wealth – might be used to pay the bills. And if they were, would taxes have to be raised by the full amount, in this century, required to cover the gap?

The answer is no. The national debt is eternal, and the future goes on forever ahead. Those debts not paid in this century can actually be rolled over into the century after that. They will provide new financial assets for future generations to hold. And while this may seem a shocking suggestion, one should realize we have been doing just exactly that with the national debt for 200 years, and no one is any worse off for it. Oh!

A few years ago, Kotlikoff evidently got the government to prepare a special analysis of the inter-generational accounting 'problem'. To his distress, the government cut the paper from the published budget in 2004. It is possible that they did this to save Bush's third tax cut, as Kotlikoff and Burns now allege. Far be it from me to defend Team Bush from any charge of improper conduct. But it is also possible that cooler heads in government just thought it better not to concede a flawed case. And it is flawed. For, in fact, the entire characterization of the Social-Security-and-Medicare problem as 'inter-generational' is misleading. It conflates and confuses two very different things: the problem of caring for today's elderly by today's young, and the problem of paying today for the future care of the elderly tomorrow. The first is a problem that must be faced today, and that will have to be faced at every future date. The second, which is what Kotlikoff and Burns want you to worry about, is an illusion.

Today's population, whether young or old, cannot set aside resources to pay real benefits or provide medical services five, ten, or twenty years from now. All we can do is make promises, as we have done, that certain benefits will be paid and services provided. When the time comes, each year's needs are met, well or poorly, by production in that year. Only a few things can be stored over long times, and medical care, personal services, and food are not among them.

Moreover, the growing older generation will be with us, whether they are cared for by Social Security and Medicare or not. If they are not, some will be cared for (up to some point) by their children. Those without children will suffer. And children without living parents will be unburdened, both financially and as a matter of conscience, relative to young people who do have aging parents to support.

The real transfer effected, every year, by Social Security and Medicare is not from today's young to tomorrow's old. And it is not even from today's young to today's old, since much of that transfer would occur in any event. It is, rather, from children without parents to children with parents. And it is from seniors with children to seniors without them. In this way, past work is honored, irrespective of reproductive choices and luck. And current virtue (the child who would care for her parents anyway) is not punished. Rather, the basic needs and medical care of all the elderly are taken care of out of a common fund.

You cannot imagine the cruelty of family life in America if Social Security and Medicare did not exist. And this is why it is hard to fathom the folly of Kotlikoff and Burns, in their argument that these two programs should be gradually abolished.

Kotlikoff and Burns would replace Social Security by a personally funded pension system with greatly reduced benefits, undoubtedly increasing poverty and insecurity among the old. They would replace Medicare with a weird voucher scheme for private medical insurance, which would require the government to keep complete and timely records of everyone's health. They would abolish the payroll tax and impose a national sales tax, spreading the burden of paying for their own retirement benefits to the elderly themselves, and also to the non-working poor. As in a Bushite's wet dream, no tax they propose would touch the cash holdings of the idle rich.

What actually should be done? Social Security should be left alone. Yes, the Trust Funds will run down as the baby boomers retire. That was the intention of the Greenspan Commission back in 1983. Social Security can perfectly well be funded partly from general revenue, which means that the burden of paying for retirees would be spread beyond workers to those with higher incomes, including the elderly who have financial wealth. What's wrong with that? Nothing. If it is politically prudent to 'keep the Trust Fund solvent', then Congress could credit the estate tax, plus income tax paid on Social Security benefits, to the Trust Fund. Assuming the estate tax is not repealed, those two measures would go a long way to filling what is, in any event, a purely cosmetic gap.

Medicare does have a problem. But it is the larger problem of American health care. The problem is that we lack a rational system to decide who gets what and how much is to be paid. The fact that America spends 14 percent of our enormous GDP on health care is, actually, a marvel, guaranteeing the possibility of first-class service to everyone. It would be better, of course, if everyone had decent insurance, if there were adequate coverage for prescription drugs, if we did not waste 3 percent out of the 14 on financial paperwork. But Medicare itself is not the source of those issues; indeed Medicare is by far the most efficient part of the health care system we do have. Cutting actual medical spending in half – merely to eliminate the so-called 'Medicare deficit' – just as the population ages and requires more care would not be a good idea.

Can the economy of the United States really, truly support its future elderly in reasonable comfort, over the years and decades to come?

Kotlikoff and Burns say no. They argue – or appear to argue on page 98 – that average real wages (the incomes of the young) will fall by 10 percent by 2075, thanks to the huge tax burdens that meeting Social Security and Medicare obligations will impose. Unless, that is, Social Security and Medicare are themselves retired. That sounds terrible.

But, as those of us who attended Kotlikoff's seminar in Texas eventually learned, that projected real wage cut is not from current levels. It is, rather, from projected levels, which include an allowance for productivity change and real wage growth. In their book, Kotlikoff and Burns mention a 1.7 percent annual productivity gain, and they concede that this will be built into growing real wages. If that holds, then in 2075 workers would be 3.3 times richer on average than today. This is on the assumption that Social Security and Medicare are killed off as recommended, and that today's boomers die miserable and poor. And, if nothing is done? If we continue to pay the terrible price of supporting tomorrow's elderly in modest comfort as we now promise to do? Well, then, according to these same assumptions, tomorrow's workers would still be three times richer than today's. Put that way, the future doesn't look so bad. But Kotlikoff and Burns never spell this out in *The Coming Generational Storm*.

(*The Texas Observer*, summer books issue, 13 August 2004)

Social Security Scare Campaign

Will Bush this week once again put Social Security privatization – or something close to it – into the headlines? Maybe he will. Maybe he won't. But one doesn't have to read tea leaves to know it's on his agenda.

The ground has been carefully prepared. New books by Peter G. Peterson – the relentless Cassandra whose thirty-years' war against Social Security can wear down skepticism even here at *Salon* – and by Laurence Kotlikoff and Scott Burns are softening up opinion leaders (see my not-very-favorable review in the *Texas Observer* [The previous chapter in this volume]).

More important, Alan Greenspan is again neglecting his day job to lend respectability to a scare campaign. Speaking to the annual Federal Reserve retreat in Jackson Hole this weekend, Greenspan spoke of 'abrupt and painful' changes required to both Social Security and Medicare, arguing that the seventy-seven million baby boomers set to retire simply pose too great a burden.

Here is what Greenspan said:

> If we have promised more than our economy has the ability to deliver, as I fear we may have, we must recalibrate our public programs so that pending retirees have time to adjust through other channels.

Friends and readers, please look carefully at that sentence. Please stop to think. First there is the conditional: 'If we have promised more than *our economy* has the ability to deliver . . .'

What have we promised? A life of luxury and decadence? It is not the case. Social Security offers a life of modest comfort to most – not

208

all – elderly Americans, as well as a system of support for survivors and the disabled. Medicare offers the elderly access to decent medical care. That is all.

Can this truly be more than 'our economy' has the ability to deliver?

Greenspan's position is that we as a country – as an economy – cannot physically afford to keep our growing elderly population out of poverty. It is that 'we' cannot afford to let 'them' see doctors when they are sick. Leaving aside the weasel words 'as I fear we may have', that is what the man said. He did not say that 'the government' can't afford to do this. He said that 'the economy' can't afford it.

Mercifully, that is not true. In fact, it is complete nonsense. We are a rich country, and we can certainly find the food, the modest housing, the clothing and the doctors, nurses, and health aides required to keep our elderly out of poverty in the years ahead.

The only question is, do we want to do this or not?

Social Security and Medicare are not mainly about transferring resources from 'the young' to 'the old'. They are mainly about *who among* the elderly – and who among the sick and the disabled and young survivors – gets taken care of, and by whom. It is an issue of distribution – and almost nothing else.

What does Mr Greenspan think will happen to the seventy-seven million baby boomers if Social Security and Medicare are scaled back? Does he think we will disappear? Well, we won't. We'll be around for a while. And those of us who have children will be a burden on them – as our parents are not a burden on us, because *they* have Social Security and Medicare. Because they have it, we also have it. If we lose it, our children will pay not only for their own retirements, but also for ours. You cannot imagine the cruelty of family life that is coming, in the day when Social Security and Medicare no longer take care of the old.

And what of the elderly who don't have children? Or those whose children are poor? Or those whose children have their own medical problems? Or those whose children just won't pony up? Social Security and Medicare take care of those elderly now, based on their histories of work. Under Mr Greenspan's plan, they would be victims of a lottery based on fertility, psychology, sexual preference and family luck.

Now, there is one other way one might interpret Greenspan's conditional. *If* it were true that Social Security and Medicare were especially costly ways of providing retirement income and medical care, then he might be right. Perhaps 'the economy' couldn't really afford that.

But that isn't true either. Compared to private insurance, Social Security and Medicare are bargains. The administrative costs are tiny.

Since the government covers everybody, it spends nothing trying to decide who is insurable and who is not. And second, the administrators of these programs are civil servants. They don't have to be paid like private CEOs. If you put everybody in the country on Medicare, private health insurance would disappear and overall medical care would cost less – with no decline in the quality of service.

Is it necessary to raise taxes, in order to pay for Social Security and Medicare? For Social Security, the true answer is: we don't know yet. It's quite possible we won't need to raise taxes by a dime. Whether we will or we won't, will depend on the growth rate of the economy over the next twenty years. If we do have to raise taxes, it won't be much. And the burden needn't fall on the poor. There is no reason, in principle or in practice, why we couldn't (just for instance) preserve the estate tax and credit its revenues to the Social Security Trust Fund.

For Medicare, yes, existing payroll tax revenues do not cover future projected expenses. But, they were never supposed to. Medicare is designed to be funded, in part, by general revenues. It's designed to paid for, partly, by taxes on income, profits and wealth. Though one can hope for reform that lowers the cost of health care, there is nothing wrong with paying for it that way. And Medicare won't be bankrupt until the whole Federal Government is bankrupt. Which it is not. And even if the whole government were bankrupt, it would make more sense to blame that calamity on Bush's tax cuts or Missile Defense, rather than on Medicare. After all, medical care for the elderly is essential. The tax cuts and Missile Defense were, and remain, unnecessary.

Let me say it again. If we have a financial problem in our government, the fault lies with tax and spending decisions taken by this government in 2001. It is grossly irresponsible, it is recklessly cruel, to blame the two programs most responsible for the basic comforts of America's seniors, now and in the years to come.

Now suppose, just for the sake of argument, that Mr Greenspan's conditional *were* true. Suppose that 'our economy' really cannot afford sustenance and doctors for the old. Then, consider the second half of the quoted sentence. In it, Greenspan declares that we must 'recalibrate our public programs' – Social Security and Medicare – 'so that pending retirees have time to adjust through other channels'.

What other channels exist? If you cut Social Security benefits, what will the 'pending retirees' do? Will they save more? In the first place, they mostly can't do that. Most Americans live hand to mouth, and if they do manage to save something at one point or another in their lives, they usually lose it to a medical disaster or some other life emergency long before they retire.

In the second place, saving is an alternative to spending. If American working families really did try to save more, as scolds like Peterson are forever recommending, that would wreck our main motor of economic growth. Note the AP story of August 30 on July's modest 'splurge' by consumers. The AP called it 'a hopeful sign the economy may be emerging from a summer funk'. It would be nice if that were true – and bad news if, as I suspect, it isn't. Mr Greenspan's idea is to make unavoidable and perpetual the bad news.

But in the third place, even if we who will one day retire could, as a class, save more and provide privately for our own retirements, that would still be an *economic* channel. Whether financed by public programs or private savings, the resources required to supply modest comfort and medical care are exactly the same.

Of *non-economic* channels, I can think of only three. Prayer. Suffering. And death. What exact combination of these Mr Greenspan prefers, he did not make clear at Jackson Hole.

(*Salon*, 31 August 2004)

Apocalypse Not Yet

With the euro touching $1.33 and the pound so high I couldn't bear to look at the rate, thought on a flight home from across the pond turned painfully to the decay of the once-almighty dollar, and to the cries of fear emanating these days from Wall Street. The current jitters are no surprise; the few Keynesians left in the economics profession have long thought them overdue.[1] Here are the most important reasons why this is so:

- We have over many years worn down our trade position in the world economy, from overpowering supremacy sixty years ago, to the point where high employment in the United States generates current account deficits well over half a trillion dollars per year. We have become dependent for our living standard on the willingness of the rest of the world to accept dollar assets – stocks, bonds, and cash – in return for real goods and services, the product of hard labor by people much poorer than ourselves in return for chits that require no effort to produce.

- For decades the Western world tolerated the 'exorbitant privilege' of a dollar-reserve economy because the United States was the indispensable power, providing reliable security against communism and insurrection without intolerable violence or oppression, conditions under which many countries on this side of the Iron Curtain grew and prospered. Those rationales evaporated fifteen years ago, and the 'Global War on Terror' is not a persuasive replacement. Thus, what was once a grudging bargain with the world's stabilizing hegemon country is now widely seen as a lingering subsidy for a predator state.

- In the late 1990s, the US position was held up by the glamour of the information technology boom, which brought capital flooding in from more precarious perches in Russia, Asia, and other parts of the world. Then, as so often on other occasions in history, America was the wave of the future. But that too has turned to dust and ashes. While major gains from new technology were achieved, few now think that silicon chips are the solution to the world's economic problems, and Silicon Valley has receded to an investment backwater.

- Since 1979, China, migrating slowly from the other side of the Iron Curtain, has become one of our largest trading partners, while the relative position of other Third World countries (more wedded to the free market and less effectively managed) has eroded. The concentration of our manufactures trade on China and Japan means that those two countries now hold preposterous dollar reserves, and their actions substantially determine the dollar's value. However, the potential actions of other players, including Russia, India and the European Central Bank, can also have important effects.

China and Japan are constrained in their behavior by creditor's risk. If they sell dollars aggressively, the value of the remainder of their portfolio plummets and they inflict large losses on themselves. This consideration prompts caution. But everything depends on what everyone else does. The rising unpredictability of US policy – including foreign policy – doesn't help. If one major player gets wind that others may dump, then the urge to join in becomes hard to resist. This is exactly analogous to an old-fashioned stock panic or run on the bank.

The current account is strongly linked in a triangular relationship to the budget deficit and also, critically, to the savings-investment balance of American households, as readers of the invaluable strategic papers by Wynne Godley (at www.levy.org) will know. In the present environment, with households on average near financial balance, the current account and the budget deficits are nearly equal. But this does *not* mean – as leading Democrats appear to believe – that reducing the budget deficit will save the dollar. A bank, hit by a panic, cannot save itself by cutting its advertising budget, raising its fees, or firing its staff.

And once a rush gets going, jacking up interest rates won't stop it either. Small interest rate hikes do normally affect exchange rates, but only when no player has the kind of extreme market weight now enjoyed by China and Japan. When they do, reactions are unpredictable if not perverse. The Fed's moves earlier this year could well have been aimed, mainly, at deterring the Japanese and Chinese from dumping. Think of them as a petty bribe – a percent or so on a few trillion dollars. Or you might call it a reaction to blackmail, deemed expedient in view of the election. But the election is now past, and that game is up.

Now we hear rumors of Russia trading dollars for euro, of India diversifying its reserves, of China contemplating the same. The reaction on Wall Street has been a trifle unnerved. In comments relayed furiously across the Internet, Morgan Stanley economist Steven Roach apparently told clients to gird for an 'economic Armageddon'. The dike, once solid, starts to crack; none can say just where or when it will break. But the little Dutch boy, Alan Greenspan, went to Frankfurt a few days back and plainly stated that he did not have enough fingers.

The most stunning aspect of these events has been the insouciance of the Bush Administration. Neither the President, nor Secretary of the Treasury John Snow, nor anyone else has troubled even to emit the usual platitudes about the greenback – not, at least with the slightest conviction. It's almost as if they've figured it out. It's almost as if they realize the awful truth. Which is that the dollar's decline is mainly good for their friends, and bad mainly for those about whom they couldn't care less.

Yet that is the truth. The dollar's decline immediately boosts the stock market, for a simple reason. Multinationals have earnings in the US and in Europe. When the dollar falls, US earnings stay the same but the European earnings go up when measured in dollars. Oil prices in dollars will stay up – at least enough to prevent the price in euros from falling. This too helps US oil company profits, measured in dollars. Meanwhile, China will keep its renminbi tied to the dollar, and prices of Chinese imports won't rise much, so Wal-Mart isn't badly hurt. The American consumer will get hit, but mainly on the oil price rather than on the rest of the consumption basket. Many will grumble, but few will recognize the political roots of their problem.

Since the US owes its debts in dollars, the financial blow will fall first on China and Japan, in the form of a depreciation of their holdings. Tough luck. Latin American debtor countries will get hit on their exports, but helped on their debt service. Those (like Mexico) who export almost exclusively to the US will get squeezed; others (like Argentina) who market to Europe but pay interest in dollars will be hurt less. An unequivocal loser is Europe, which has been hoping for an export-led fix to their own, largely self-inflicted, mass unemployment. The Europeans can forget about that.

If Bush's insouciance works, the dollar *could* decline smoothly for a while and then, simply, stop declining. US exports might recover somewhat, helping manufacturing, though there's no chance exports and imports will balance. But even so, the dollar system *could* stay intact, so long as China and Japan remain willing to add new dollars to their depreciated hoard. Given that their interests lie in maintaining export activity and the jobs it creates, they may very well make that choice. Large-scale dollar purchases by the European Central Bank are also a remote possibility (the option has been mentioned on the periphery of the ECB). The problems would return later on, but meanwhile, such an action would prove that God really does look after children, small dogs and the United States.

What could up-end the apple-cart? An unstoppable panic is probably not yet the largest risk. There are simply too many dollars in the theater of the world economy, too few exits, and only a few elephantine players. The latter would soon be discouraged from selling by the soaring price of the available alternative assets, and the run would fizzle out. Thus the final dollar crisis will probably wait until a political crisis – say someday with China – sets it off.

Some fear rising long-term interest rates – and a recession – simply on account of the sliding dollar and price inflation. But this also won't necessarily happen. For an inflation premium to be built into the long-term interest rate, there needs to be higher *expected* inflation on a continuing basis. Notwithstanding the cheap psychology of 'rational expectations', beloved of economists, actual inflation can rise for a long time before expectations do. And the inflation adjustment, coming (let us say) primarily through a rising dollar oil price, could come and go rather quickly. It need not get built into a spiral of wages and prices. So far, despite the substantial dollar decline that has already occurred, long-term interest rates have hardly budged. They have generally risen no more, and in some cases less, than the short-term rates Greenspan started pushing up last spring.

A change in European policy – toward a high-growth, full employment Keynesianism – could bring a decisive shift in the world balance of economic power. Such a shift would create profits in Europe (where there presently are few), attracting capital. It would open up a European current account deficit, where there is presently a surplus. Soon the euro would not be a scarce currency any longer, and the reduction of the dollar's reserve status could truly get under way. Unfortunately for Europeans, European policymakers don't see – and won't seize – this opportunity. Frankly they are too reactionary and too stupid. That's a tragedy for Europe, though in some ways it's undeserved good luck for the United States.

And the fourth possibility is that Alan Greenspan could change his mind, raise interest rates and inflict on us all a monumental 'defense of the dollar'. Morgan's Roach worries about this with some good reason; I've worried about it too. While sharply rising interest rates could cure both inflation and the weak dollar – as they did in the early 1980s – the resulting slump would be even more disastrous than it was then, because debt levels are higher now than they were. Just as the slump then destroyed Latin American and Africa, a new one could bring China, Japan, India and others into worldwide recession. There would be no easy way out.

Such folly is possible but now I don't expect it. I rather think Greenspan will take a pass on all the past decades of Federal Reserve myth-making. That means, that he will actually sit on his hands while oil and some other import prices drive upward. Given the alternatives, it's probably the right course of action. But let no one say, afterward and with a straight face, that our Central Bank takes all that seriously the bunkum it spreads, about fighting inflation.

For this reason, we're more likely to enter a strange new world, where Republicans in office behave like 1970s Democrats on meth. In a stagflation economy, budget deficits are inevitable and there is no strategy that will end them. It's obvious that adding large near-term tax increases to the mix would merely slow growth further, while there isn't enough federal public non-defense spending left to cut. So the Republicans will make excuses, and let the deficits run on, and incur the scolding of the IMF and the OECD. If we're lucky. It's far from the worst thing the Republicans could do.

Sadly the Democrats will respond as badly as possible, like 1930s Republicans on downers. In a touching devotion to dogma, they will call for fiscal discipline to close the budget deficit. This will undermine the case for relief to working families, for aid to state and local government, and the defense of Social Security benefits that they might otherwise make. Our jobless compatriots won't find this endearing. Faced with higher inflation, Democrats may demand to know why Greenspan has done nothing. Households struggling to manage their debts will not be greatly amused. Then Democrats will say that things were better under Clinton. That's thin gruel; in the 1930s you could have said the same of Coolidge.

The reality is that budget deficits *cannot* be controlled until the trade problem is fixed. So what should be done? It's a long-term project, but it's not difficult to assemble the start of a real program. Oil companies are likely to earn high profits in the turbulence ahead. Let's tax them (and other windfalls), perhaps with a variable import fee. Let's plough the proceeds back to state and local governments, so they can maintain services and vital investments. Let's cut payroll taxes for now, to help working people cope. And let's start our next technology boom, focused on new energy and reduction in per-unit GDP consumption of oil. These would be useful beginnings on the home front.

The big action, however, must come on the international side. My supply-side friends pine for the gold standard, and they make a serious point. The experiment of worldwide floating exchange rates, inaugurated by global monetarists in 1971, has failed disastrously so far as developing countries are concerned. Indeed in the most successful arena of global development we have fixed exchange rates right now, thanks to the unappreciated but sensible dollar-pegging of the Chinese. Fixing exchange rates in Europe (through the extreme measure of creating a single currency) also proved a boon for the poorer countries of Europe, eliminating speculative currency risk. Even though overall European policy remains terrible, unemployment has dropped sharply in Spain and Greece since the euro came in.

Globally-managed exchange rates would help developing countries, by sharply curtailing the destabilizing role of private currency markets. They would therefore also help us, by creating stronger and more stable markets for our exports. But there is no simple return to global fixed exchange rates. It would be a terrible mistake to create a system that imposed deflationary pressure on us and through us on the world as a whole – the problem of the classical gold standard. To get where we need to go, we must also recreate a global financial network oriented toward the support of development and growth. When we have that, growth policies around the world will help rather than hurt each other. At that point, we could profitably put real effort into reintroducing full employment economics to Europe and Japan.

For such a policy to succeed, America must also change. Specifically we must turn away from our present over-reliance on armed forces and private bankers, far away from the fantasy of self-serving dominance for which, the markets are clearly telling us, the world will not agree to pay. We need instead an industrial strategy based on technological leadership, collective security, and smart use of the world's resources. The financial counterpart must be a new source of liquidity for many developing countries, permitting them to step up their imports, and correspondingly our exports and employment. This will probably require a new network of regional regulatory agents, empowered to enforce capital control and to take responsibility for successful development strategies among their members.

The point is not that any of this would be easy. Nor can it be done in the lifetime of this Administration or of the political dominance that Bush now seeks to achieve. The point is, rather, that there is no viable alternative, so far as I know. Absent a fully articulated strategy, the attempt to pretend otherwise with a few slogans is an economic and also a political dead-end.

Two steps are thus required. The first is thought, and the second, when the opportunity arises, will be action. The scope of action cannot be small, for the problem now exceeds six hundred billion dollars every year. But only by dealing with it, over time, can we hope to regain full employment without witnessing, sooner or later, the final run on the dollar.

Note

1. In early 2003, I wrote this account for *Dollars and Sense:*

> the question remains: As the U.S. trade position continues to erode, will foreigners be willing to add to their holdings of dollar assets by enough to allow the U.S. to consume at levels consistent with full employment? The amount to be absorbed at present is in the range of half a trillion dollars per year. This was easily handled when dollar asset prices were rising. But now that dollar asset prices are falling, dollar assets are not as attractive as they once were. If foreigners are not willing to absorb all the dollars we need to place, and if asset prices do not quickly fall to the point where U.S. stocks appear cheap, dollar dumping is, sooner or later, inevitable.

(TomPaine.com, 6 December 2004)

Taming Predatory Capitalism

In 1899 Thorstein Veblen described predation as a phase in the evolution of culture, 'attained only when the predatory attitude has become the habitual and accredited spiritual attitude ... when the fight has become the dominant note in the current theory of life'. After an entire century's struggle to escape from this phase, we've suffered a relapse. The predators are everywhere unleashed; the institutions built to contain them, from the UN to the AFL-CIO to the SEC, are everywhere under siege. Predation has become again the defining feature of economic life; our first problem is to grasp this reality in full.

Postwar prosperity was built on a vast cut in the cost of security, achieved by stable distribution of power among nation-states. The world of warring empires and restive colonies disappeared; Europe discovered it could thrive without them. Peace worked in the poor countries too: the rise of China and India owes much to those countries having enjoyed it since 1979; likewise in much of Southeast Asia. But in Africa and the Middle East war remains an absolute barrier to development. The American role in the Cold War system was to provide security; for this the dollar's role as anchor of the world trading system was our reward. But now, with Iraq, we are seen worldwide as the leading predator state, promoting war as a solution rather than as the ultimate economic and human horror. For this, many would like to see our privileges revoked.

Corporate and financial fraud and political corruption form the second great domain of predatory capitalism. DeLay, Frist and Abramoff are the names in the news, but the tone is set by the leadership, Cheney of Halliburton and Bush of Harken Energy – a large predator and a small scavenger, specialized in cronyism and expert in nothing else. When predation becomes the dominant business and political

219

form – and who can deny this? – the foundation of capitalism crumbles. Markets lose legitimacy, investors fly to safety in bonds, and authentic innovation and shared growth both become unattainable under the system. The solution must be not just a change of parties but a new political class, including a new media not under corrupt control.

Then there is the predatory attack on unions and labor, in which many economists are complicit. This is far advanced in America and most visible today in Europe, spearheaded by the doctrine of flexible labor markets, which claims that the conquest of unemployment requires cutting the pay of the working poor. But there is no history of unemployment ever being conquered this way – certainly not in the US of the 1940s, 1960s or 1990s. Modern Europe also affords counter-examples of equalizing growth, from Norway and Denmark to recent gains in Spain, as well as object lessons, most recently in France, of the catastrophe of designed exclusion.

The way forward is a program for growth and justice, built on the needs of the working population and the middle class. To begin with in the United States, there must be a powerful demolition of the old political order: elections where all votes are cast and counted. The campaign against vote repression is the essential civil rights struggle of our time, even though most progressives don't seem to realize it yet. Prevailing will require fundamental reform such as the introduction of nationwide vote-by-mail (the Oregon system). Without that, and also many relentless prosecutions, nothing else will be achieved.

The economic commitment, in turn, must be to full employment here, to egalitarian growth in Europe and Japan, and to a worldwide development strategy favoring civil infrastructure and the poor. Public capital investment, stronger unions and a high minimum wage should frame the domestic agenda. Overseas, crackdowns on tax havens and the arms trade, a stabilizing financial system and an end to the debt peonage of poor countries should be among the high priorities of a new structure.

The truths are that egalitarian growth is efficient, that speculation must be regulated, that crime starts at the top, and that peace is the primary public good. These truths are poison to predators and the reason they have fostered and subsidized an entire cynical intellectual movement devoted to 'free' markets, a class of professor-courtiers now everywhere in view. Taming predatory capitalism could start with breaking this econo-corporate analytical axis, and reviving the concept of countervailing power, first formulated by John Kenneth Galbraith in 1952.

(*The Nation*, March 2006)

Index